# The Beggar's Opera

Mr Gay

# The Beggar's Opera

## *Its Predecessors and Successors*

*By* FRANK KIDSON

**GREENWOOD PRESS, PUBLISHERS**
WESTPORT, CONNECTICUT

*To my friend*
*A L F R E D  M O F F A T*
*in memory of Auld Lang Syne*

Originally published in 1922
by Cambridge University Press, Cambridge, England

First Greenwood Reprinting 1971

Library of Congress Catalogue Card Number 72-109760

SBN 8371-4250-4

Printed in the United States of America

# PREFACE

TO the late Victorian *The Beggar's Opera* is but a name; to his father or grandfather it may have been a memory of some imperfect representation—perhaps as cut down to an after-piece —given at a provincial theatre.

Apart from its dramatic appeal, the opera quickly became a classic. Its vigour, its picturesqueness, its unfolding of a bygone life, its association with Pope, Swift, and others of that coterie have made it of permanent interest to the literary man.

This little volume aims at presenting in a handy form such facts as bear upon the inception of Gay's masterpiece and its influence upon the English stage; and secondly at giving a brief account of the Italian operas that preceded it and of the ballad operas for which it led the way.

The recent production has caused a renewed interest in *The Beggar's Opera* and given to the twentieth century a glimpse of the dramatic art which delighted generations of our ancestors.

F. K.

May, 1922.

# CONTENTS

# ILLUSTRATIONS

## Illustrations

# THE *BEGGAR'S* OPERA

## INTRODUCTION

THE perennial success of *The Beggar's Opera*, which has retained its popularity for nearly a couple of centuries, forms a record in dramatic productions. The causes of this popularity have varied with each generation, and the original source of its favour has long ago been lost and given place to one quite different from what the author expected or perhaps desired. It is very doubtful if John Gay saw more in his work than an ephemeral satire on passing phases of the day. He could not have foretold that the piece would run even the sixty-three nights of the season at Lincoln's Inn Theatre, and, while he may have expected that some abuse would be hurled at the satire contained in the opera, he certainly did not think that the creation of Macheath, his gang, and women followers would be denounced as incentives to vice and immorality. It has been the fate of *The*

*Beggar's Opera* to draw forth much mistaken invective, while the lesson which Gay undoubtedly wished to teach was ignored or unnoticed.

I have said that the causes which have made the piece such a favourite with all classes and with generations that have widely differed in thought were many, and it is my task in the following pages, before dealing with the opera itself, to try to realise them for the reader. In view of this it becomes necessary to refer to the state of the musical drama in England during the reigns of Queen Anne and of George I, with some notice of earlier productions.

In the early part of the eighteenth century that portion of the nation which ever sought its musical art from other countries welcomed opera as it appeared on the Italian stage, and applauded its transfer to the English boards with all its company of foreign exponents. This class of opera was in full swing when Gay offered his piece to the public. The 'man in the street' was silent and to a certain extent uncatered for. He kept away from the Italian operas and confessed that they were things he could not understand or appreciate at their true value—if value they had. At any rate he had little sympathy with what he called the 'squallings' of these foreign men and women in a language which he did not understand and to music of which he had an equally poor opinion. *The Beggar's Opera* had an appeal to the ordinary man not only for its wit, its satire, its picturesqueness, but, musically, for the pretty, simple airs that were plentifully besprinkled throughout it. Every man and woman could sing them, and that they were favourites, apart from their place in the opera, is shown by the popularity of many of them for a century and a half after their original publication. Of such airs as 'Cease your funning' instrumental arrangements are plentiful among the music sheets of sixty or seventy years ago, and the lively melody 'If the heart of a man is depressed with cares' was kept alive in Victorian drawing-rooms by its use for the 'bowing figure' in the Lancers.

The great run of the opera's recent revival at Hammersmith, with its touring companies and full houses wherever performed, shows how ready we of the twentieth century are to appreciate its pictures of old-time life, its old-time satire, its quaint dresses, picturesque dances, and sparkling music, simple though that music be. *The Beggar's Opera* is so much of a classic that we may easily grant that the present run will not end its career on the English stage, and we may expect revival after revival, each possibly with what may be termed a 'new reading' as each actor-manager sees it in his own light. He would be a vandal indeed who would tamper with its music, but who can tell whether or no such vandal may arise? In the course of its passage down to our time the opera has had its ordeals, and actors and managers have played not very kindly tricks with it. Fortunately for the present day representation, the producers have gone to the original source and discarded modern innovations and omissions. For the piece has suffered its martyrdom at the hands of country managers of stock companies, who have used it in their need for after-pieces and other exigences. There were no acting fees to pay, no author to appease for the mutilation of the piece. Like Shakespeare's work, it was common property and was able to stand all the ignominy that such persons put upon it and to sustain its effect in spite of inartistic tamperings. Managers always found it a safe 'draw,' no matter whether Polly could, or could not, sing the airs allotted to her; whether or no Macheath was inadequate, the piece drew its audience in every provincial theatre a hundred and less years ago.

Popular songs of the day were interpolated and little heed taken of the unities of the story, and every budding Polly Peachum, no doubt knowing of the good fortune of her predecessor in the past, dreamed silently of the duke who was going to take her from the stage. Lavinia Fenton was an unknown woman, young and pretty perhaps, but chance turned her into a duchess, and so.... But no duke after that of Bolton sought a Polly Peachum of a later date, and the Pollies of the provincial stage had to be content with what fortune granted them.

## OPERA IN ENGLAND PRIOR TO
### *THE BEGGAR'S OPERA*

EFORE we can fully realise the enormous influence *The Beggar's Opera* had upon the English stage in regard to musical pieces, it will be necessary to deal, at least briefly, with the musical drama before Gay's production was staged.

How the English stage became overridden by foreign productions is one of those mysteries that will never be solved. The sturdy English character which was supposed to prevail in the eighteenth century and to repudiate 'anything foreign' was not greatly in evidence among the more cultured, for this class accepted without a murmur—save one of satisfaction—foreign music, foreign singers, foreign dancing-masters, and much that was really alien to the nation.

In the reign of Elizabeth and in that of James I masques were a great feature in Court entertainments. They were performed also at Lincoln's Inn, Gray's Inn, and similar places, while equally elaborate ones were done at the houses of the nobles. Ben Jonson was author of many of these masques, and the notable *Comus*, written by John

Milton for his friend Henry Lawes, shows us the type that was in vogue. Milton's *Comus* was written for an entertainment at the house of the Earl of Bridgewater and performed by his children and their music-master, Henry Lawes, in 1634. How Thomas Augustine Arne, then a young man, in 1738 wrote fresh music to Milton's words (with additions to the words by Dr Dalton), and the exquisite quality and beauty of that music, are matters perhaps outside the present essay. It is sufficient to know that the masques of the sixteenth and seventeenth centuries were dressed in costume, and had scenery, properties, and music. Each had a plot, frequently founded on some classic story or legend. That of *Comus* was founded upon the incident of one of the Earl's children being lost in a wood. How much these masques differed from the operas of later date is not very clear; at any rate, the dividing-line cannot have been very definite or certain.

During the Commonwealth (in 1642) stage-plays were prohibited, and the musical, as well as the legitimate, drama was under a cloud. At the same time private musical entertainments of the order of masque or opera were in vogue to a limited degree. At this time the opera in Italy was in a very flourishing state and had taken a particular and well-understood form.

Sir William Davenant had been the producer of many masques and musical entertainments, and he obtained permission from Cromwell to open a semi-private theatre at Rutland House for the performance of these and similar pieces. One was *The first dayes Entertainment at Rutland House, by declamations and musick after the manner of the ancients.* This was performed in 1656, and as the words were in Italian the Protector very sagely allowed it because he opined it could have no harmful influence, being in a language not generally understood. The music for this piece, whatever its character, was supplied by Henry Lawes, Dr Charles Coleman, Henry Cooke, and George Hudson. It has been asserted that this was the first attempt at opera in England, but it is doubtful whether it can be ranked as one; a stronger claim can be made for another of Sir William Davenant's productions, *The Siege of Rhodes.* This was acted at the semi-private theatre at Rutland House, Charterhouse Square, in 1656. It was again acted at a theatre which Davenant opened in Lincoln's Inn Fields. In this perform-ance more elaborate setting was given, with a second part added. After the Restoration John Evelyn, under the date January 9th, 1662, records that he saw the second part of *The Siege of Rhodes.*

The printed libretto of *The Siege of Rhodes* refers to the composers who were claimed to be 'the most transcendent of England in that art, and perhaps not unequal to the best masters abroad.' The audience are informed that the music is 'recitative and therefore unpractised here, though of great reputation amongst other nations.' The composers were H. Lawes, Matthew Lock, Dr Coleman, H. Cooke, and G. Hudson.

Of the many masques and musical entertainments that Davenant produced, the above-named *Siege of Rhodes* appears to have been the most famous and the most popular. He followed this success by *The Cruelty of the Spaniards in Peru.* This was in 1658, and Evelyn saw it on May 5th, 1659. He describes it as 'a new opera after the Italian way in recitative music and scenes, much inferior to the Italian composure and magnificence; but it was prodigious that in a time of such public consternation such a vanity should be kept up or permitted.'

It was in Davenant's pieces that female actors are said to have been first seen on the stage. Both he and his son, Dr Charles Davenant, must be given credit for their activity in producing musical plays and, as it were, paving the way for the operas and musical dramas that Henry Purcell glorified by his music.

But Davenant, although he led the way, was not the only producer of musical plays or operas at this period. James Shirley's interlude, *The Contention of Ajax and Ulysses* (1659), and a musical drama, *The Marriage of Ocean and Britannia*, by Richard Flecknoe (1659), were two that may be classed as operas or masques. Shirley wrote a number of masques and interludes which were produced between 1633 and 1659. The brothers William and Henry Lawes chiefly supplied the music.

When Charles II came to the throne in 1660 the ban on the theatre was removed, and his known taste in theatrical performances and music gave great encouragement to the drama, musical and otherwise.

It is not my purpose to follow closely the record of the musical drama in England before *The Beggar's Opera* saw the light, but a general idea of what had been the staple fare in this class of work may be useful in understanding what a great revolution Gay's opera made, and how these pieces of the pre-Restoration and Restoration periods led up to the operas that John Gay ridiculed.

As is well-known, Charles, during his absence from England, had acquired a French taste in art, especially in that of music. He brought over with him to his Court a number of French performers and, in imitation of the twenty-four fiddlers of the King of France, instituted a similar band of violinists under the leadership of John Banister.

But high in the favour of Charles was one Lewis Grabu, a Frenchman, who had come over to England with his royal master. Whatever Charles II thought of Grabu's compositions, the common verdict of a later age, and indeed that of his own, is not very favourable. Grabu was a personage at Court and essayed one or two musical dramas which fell very flat indeed. The first of these was a sort of opera called *Ariadne, or The Marriage of Bacchus*. This was translated from the French and performed by 'the gentlemen of the Academy of Music.'

But the work that he is best remembered by is *Albion and Albanius, an Opera, or Representation in Musick*. It was 'Set by Lewis Grabu, Esquire, Master of his late Majesty's Musick,' and published in a fine folio volume in 1687, 'For the Author, and to be sold at the door of the Royal Theater.' The words of this piece were by John Dryden and dealt in allegory with the troubles 'of two princes united in common sufferings from ungrateful and rebellious subjects.' Charles died before Grabu had published his work and it was dedicated to his royal brother, James II.

The opera is in three acts and of enormous

length, and is as uninteresting a piece of work as
may be found. 'Albion' and 'Albanius' are the
thinly disguised names for Charles and his brother,
the Duke of York, and the opera refers to the
different plots and oppositions that the two princes
had to face. It was acted at the Duke's Theatre
in 1685, after the death of Charles II. It was
well mounted, but it fell remarkably flat; and
during its sixth performance, on the 13th of June,
1685, the audience broke up in confusion, as the
news of Monmouth's invasion had just then
reached London.

Dryden gives a useful description of opera as
understood in his day. He says: 'An Opera is a
poetical tale or fiction, represented by vocal and
instrumental music, adorned with scenes, machines,
and dancing. The supposed persons of this musical
drama are generally supernatural, as gods, and
goddesses, and heroes, which at least are descended
from them, and are in due time to be adopted into
their number. The subject, therefore, being ex-
tended beyond the limits of human nature, admits
of that sort of marvellous and surprising conduct
which is rejected in other plays. Human impossi-
bilities are to be received as they are in faith;
because where gods are introduced, a Supreme Power
is to be understood, and second causes are out of
doors; yet propriety is to be observed even here....

Phoebus must foretell, Mercury must charm with his caduceus, and Juno must reconcile the quarrels of the marriage bed. To conclude, they must all act according to their distinct and peculiar characters.' Dryden here gives an excellent epitome of the rules which governed the Italian and Anglo-Italian operas of the late seventeenth and early eighteenth centuries. If the operas were founded upon the Italian classic romances and legends, the chief feature that was preserved throughout the whole piece was the heroic character. When we realise this and remember how Gay brought his opera into common-place life— nay, into the degraded life of a prison, with characters taken from its lowest phase—thieves, receivers of stolen goods, and women of the town —we can well understand what a supreme blow he gave to the mock heroics and high-falutin speech and action that made up the operas which he ridiculed. Dryden paid a great tribute of admiration to Lewis Grabu which nobody appears to have seconded. His royal master, Charles, was dead, and James, the succeeding king, was probably not so enthusiastic over the French musician as his elder brother. Grabu remained in obscurity, but in 1690 he composed the incidental music to Waller's alterations of Beaumont and Fletcher's *Maid's Tragedy*.

It was now that Henry Purcell arose to redeem the music of the English opera from the poor stuff that had hitherto held the ground. John Dryden was one of the principal writers for the musical dramas of his day, while others were Nahum Tate, Thomas D'Urfey, Mrs Behn, and a few more.

The first effort of Purcell in the style of opera was *Dido and Æneas.* The libretto is in rhyme, written by Nahum Tate, the versifier of the Psalms. The occasion of its production was this. The proprietor of a young gentlewomen's boarding school in Leicester Fields, who afterwards removed to Chelsea, was Mr Josias Priest, a dancing master and composer of stage dances. His connection with the theatre naturally inclined him towards a dramatic representation to be enacted by the young ladies under his charge. Henry Purcell, then a young man, who had already been recognised sufficiently to be made organist at Westminster Abbey, was commissioned to write music to Nahum Tate's libretto. The date of this is by no means settled. Early authorities give it as 1675, but later researches seem to point to a date seven or eight years later. The opera appears to have remained in manuscript, except for certain transcripts, until it was published in full by the Musical Antiquarian Society in 1841 under the editorship of G. Alexander Macfarren.

The music which Henry Purcell composed for the dramatic pieces of his day was great in quantity. No doubt his introduction to the theatre was due to Josias Priest, after the young composer had shown his capabilities in the music to *Dido and Æneas*. The number of dramatic pieces for which Purcell supplied the music between *Dido* and his death in 1695 amounts to nearly forty. Much of this music is merely of an incidental character, but there is some that is operatic and some that is on the border line. *The Tempest*, altered by Dryden and Sir William Davenant from Shakespeare, may claim to be opera. *Dioclesian, or the Prophetess* (1690), altered from Beaumont and Fletcher, is another piece of note, while *King Arthur* (1691) and *Bonduca*, the last composed in the last year of Purcell's life, 1695, are notable examples of his full opera style. In *The Tempest* occurs one of Purcell's most admired settings, 'Come unto these yellow sands,' while in *King Arthur* we get many a favourite lyric, such as 'Come if you dare,' 'Fairest Isle all Isles excelling,' 'Two daughters of an aged stream,' and some others. For this latter opera Dryden wrote the libretto and Josias Priest arranged the dances. It was performed in 1691 with elaborate scenery; it was well received at its original production, and was frequently performed in the following century. A notable adaptation of it, with a performance, occurred in 1770, when Dr Arne revived it at Drury Lane Theatre with some additions by himself. It was again revived in 1781, 1784, 1803, and 1842.

In 1692 Dryden's play, *The Indian Queen*, was turned into an opera with added songs. Purcell's fine song 'I attempt from love's sickness to fly' is found in this, as well as 'Ye twice ten hundred Deities.' *The Fairy Queen*, adapted from Shakespeare's *Midsummer Night's Dream*, is also a notable Purcell opera.

It is not my intention to dwell upon the great subject of Purcell's operas or his music for dramatic pieces. The subject is so large and so full of interest that it has been dealt with by writers on musical history in a very full manner. Suffice it to repeat that *Bonduca*, a tragedy altered from Beaumont and Fletcher, was put into operatic form by Purcell and composed in 1695, the year of the composer's death, and brought out in the next year. It contains several songs that had a separate popularity, such as 'To arms, to arms, your ensigns straight display,' and the well-known catch 'Jack thou'rt a toper.'

After the death of Purcell the English opera declined. Although there were still living some contemporaries of Purcell who were well able to continue his work, yet, from some cause or another, they do not appear to have sustained the English opera to any extent. This left room for a number of indifferent foreign musicians to place upon the stage operas either wholly of Italian origin or founded upon the Italian model. It is this succession of Italian, and Anglo-Italian, operas that Gay appears to have had in mind when he determined to bring the class into ridicule. Opera now languished in England for a few years —for England we must really say London, because at this early period the provinces do not appear to have made any attempt towards regular concerts, much less dramatic entertainments.

It was in 1705 that Italian opera first gained a footing in England, under the auspices of Thomas Clayton. This musician, of mean talents, was one of the King's band from 1692 to 1702. He went to Italy and studied there, and, returning with some knowledge of the Italian method of opera, produced one of his own composition or, more properly, of his own compilation. He had brought from Italy certain operatic songs, and with the aid of one Peter Motteux, who wrote the English words (apparently a more or less free translation of an Italian opera), made a concoction of plot and songs with an English dress into an opera with the title *Arsinoe, Queen of Cyprus*. He produced

this with the aid of Nicola Francesco Haym and
Charles Dieupart. It was performed at Drury
Lane on the 16th of January, 1705, with English
singers of note. These included Mrs Tofts, Mrs
Cross, and Mrs Lyndsay, while the male vocalists
were Leveridge, Hughes, and Cook. Clayton had
sufficient confidence in himself to proclaim his
work of the best, and for a brief period the public
took him at his own valuation. All writers agree,
however, that the opera was contemptible both as
regards words and music. It ran for twenty-four
nights in the first season and for eleven in the
next. In regarding the 'runs' of the successful
pieces in the eighteenth century and comparing
them with the prolonged successes of our own
day one wonders how these admittedly lengthy
eighteenth century runs ever paid for the cost of
scenery, vocalists' fees, and all the expenses that
belong to the theatre. *The Beggar's Opera*'s run
of sixty-three nights appeared to be such a startling
event in those days as to have been dwelt upon as
a record.

There had arrived in England Margharita de
l'Epine, an Italian lady, who at once made her
mark as a singer of the highest class. She was
accustomed to sing Italian songs, and she sang
some of these between the acts of *Arsinoe*. It is
said that there was much rivalry between Mrs

Tofts and herself. Margharita, though possessed
of musical abilities far beyond the ordinary, was
not greatly favoured by nature as regards looks.
She retired from the stage in 1718 after having
sung in a number of Italian operas that had been
put upon the British boards, and married Dr
Pepusch, strangely enough the man who arranged
Gay's opera. Margharita de l'Epine was not only
a vocalist of great merit but a skilful harpsichord
player, as is shown by the Fitzwilliam Virginal
Manuscript which belonged to Dr Pepusch, and
from which she was wont to play. Anyone who
has turned over the pages of the original manuscript and seen the closely written music will
realise the difficulty of the feat.

Joseph Addison appears to have regarded Clayton as a musical genius and allowed him to set
music to a dramatic piece which he had written, *Rosamond*, founded upon the story of Fair
Rosamond and Queen Eleanor. This was performed on March 4th, 1707. The music was so
utterly mediocre that it killed all belief in Clayton's
skill in the art. Thomas Augustine Arne reset
*Rosamond*, his first great work, in 1733. So far
as we may judge from the published detached
songs (for it never appears to have been issued in
its entirety), Arne's music was tuneful and delightful. 'Was ever nymph like Rosamond so fair'

was sung by Arne's sister, who took the title rôle, while his younger brother was a page. The piece was performed in March, 1733.

To revert to the Italian opera which absorbed the English stage, *Camilla* was the next opera after the Italian model. It was produced at Drury Lane on the 30th of April, 1706. It was a direct translation from the Italian by Owen McSwiney, then manager of Drury Lane. The music was by Marc Antonio Buononcini. It was performed by the same company as *Arsinoe*, and was well liked by the Town; it was repeated in the following year. In *Camilla* the celebrated singer Nicolini, whose full name was Nicolini Grimaldi, made his first appearance on the English stage. A native of Naples, he sang in most of the Anglo-Italian operas. *Camilla* was performed half in English and half in Italian, the Italian singers, including Margharita de l'Epine, singing in their native tongue, and the English singers in theirs. The part of the heroine, Camilla, was sung by Mrs Tofts, who made a great success of it and won universal praise. She retired from the stage, mentally afflicted, in 1709, in the height of her fame, and died in 1760.

*Thomyris, Queen of Scythia* was an opera after the Italian manner written by Peter Motteux with the music supplied from the existing airs of

Scarlatti and Buononcini. These were put into form and adapted by Dr Pepusch. The opera was performed at Drury Lane in the autumn of 1707 and with renewed splendour in the following year. The singers were Italian and English who each sang in their own language.

A succeeding opera was *Pyrrhus and Demetrius,* translated from the Italian by Manager McSwiney. The music of the original was by Alessandro Scarlatti, and this was adapted to the English version of the words by Nicola Haym, who added an overture and some additional airs. It was acted on December 14th, 1708, and met with approval. The music is of a quality far exceeding that of Clayton's effort. As in *Camilla,* the singers were of mixed nationality and sang in their respective tongues. The bulk of the public did not seem to mind this extraordinary method of vocalising an opera—they accepted it as part of the plan.

The performance of *Pyrrhus* is mentioned by Sir Richard Steele in the fourth number of *The Tatler.* After saying that a great part of the opera was done in Italian, he tells us that 'a great critic fell into fits in the gallery at feeling, not only time and place, but language and nations confused in the most incorrigible manner....He has...considered the nature of sounds in general, and made a very elaborate digression upon the London cries, where-

in he has shown from reason and philosophy why
oysters are cried, card-matches sung, and turnips
and all other vegetables neither cried, sung, nor
said, but sold, with an accent and tone neither
natural to man or beast.'

*Pyrrhus and Demetrius* was the last opera sung
bilingually, the succeeding operas being rendered
entirely in Italian and as a consequence the English singers were dismissed in favour ·of Italians.
The loss to the opera stage of such singers as
Leveridge, Mrs Tofts, and others was of course
great.

In 1710 was first acted the opera *Almahide*, the
supposed work of Buononcini. This was sung
entirely in Italian by the singers who had invaded
the English stage and replaced the sturdy English
voices by artificially produced ones. The next
opera to follow was *Hydaspes*. In this Nicolini
took the part of Hydaspes. The plot of the opera
was dramatic enough. Hydaspes, the brother of
Artaxerxes, King of Persia, is a rival to the King
in the affections of Princess Berenice. His brother
condemns Hydaspes to be devoured by a lion in
the amphitheatre while Berenice is placed to see
her lover's sufferings. Hydaspes with much vocal
effort begs the lion, which is supposed not to see
him at first, to 'come on.' The lion, who must
have been a very tame 'super,' accepts the chal-

lenge and there is a struggle, Hydaspes and the
lion pausing in the combat while Hydaspes declares
his love for Berenice and explains matters generally in florid Italian singing. Hydaspes strangles
the lion and, setting his foot on the beast in sign
of victory, asks if any other monster is available.
The people call for Hydaspes to be saved from
other lions and he is released from a perilous
position, all ending happily. The lion incident
seemed to provoke a good deal of good-natured
satire, and Addison in *The Spectator* pokes fun
at Nicolini's struggles with it. The opera was by
Francesco Mancini and it was acted in 1710.

The Italian opera was now about to undergo a
great change. Handel, who had made a reputation
for himself on the Continent and was Master of
the Chapel to the Elector of Hanover, had been
invited to England by several noblemen and lovers
of music. He came over towards the end of the
year 1710, without any design to settle in this
country. Aaron Hill, who had the management
of the Haymarket Theatre, at once sought him
out and prevailed upon him to write an opera for
his theatre. Hill suggested the plan of taking as subject the episode of Rinaldo and Armida from Tasso's
*Jerusalem Delivered*. The libretto was written by
Rossi, a poet of some merit who was employed
afterwards upon the libretti of other Italian operas.

Handel was so quick with his work that it is stated that he composed the whole of the music in a fortnight. The piece was performed on the 24th of February, 1711, and was an instant success, audiences quickly seeing how superior was the music of the new composer to that of the Italian operas that preceded it.

The libretto was entirely in Italian, and the Italian vocalists who had sung in the earlier operas were employed along with certain others who were in the service of the Elector of Hanover. Dr Burney says that in the original score, though not in the printed copies, was a symphony of twenty-one bars for octave-flutes in imitation of the song of birds. By what was no doubt esteemed at the time a very happy idea, a number of sparrows were let loose. Whether Handel was party to this stage trick or not there is no record. Addison in *The Spectator* takes notice of this particular point in the opera. In the fifth number (6th of March, 1711) he, in the character of Mr Spectator, speaks of having met a fellow with a cage of sparrows on his shoulder. He elicits the information that they are for the opera, to be let loose at the end of the first act. He is jocular over the circumstance and speaks of a design to cast the story of Dick Whittington into an opera and to let loose a number of mice as the sparrows were;

but he tells us that, when it was thus proposed, Mr Rich, the proprietor of the Play House, objected that the single cat of Whittington could not finish off the lot, and so this excellent idea came to naught. Mr Spectator concludes: 'I hear there is a treaty on foot with London and Wise (who will be appointed gardeners of the Play House) to furnish the opera of *Rinaldo and Armida* with an orange grove; and that the next time it is acted the singing birds will be personated by tom tits, the undertakers being resolved to spare neither pains nor money for the gratification of their audiences.'

The opera, as by 'Signor Hendel,' was published by John Walsh and John Hare in folio. Walsh is said to have made a profit of fifteen hundred pounds by his publication, which led to Handel's remark: 'You shall compose the next opera and I will publish it.' Whether this is a true or a false anecdote, there is little doubt but that the composer would have as small a share in the profits of the production as any one concerned.

The advent of Handel in Italian opera seems to have placed on the shelf the prior Italian productions and to have prevented any further supply for the English stage. *Rinaldo* appears to have been as elaborately staged as the earlier Italian operas. That these had elaborate scenery and 'machinery,' as it was called, is shown by Addison's article in *The Spectator* from which I have already made a quotation. 'An opera,' he says, 'may be allowed to be extravagantly lavish in its decorations, as its only design is to gratify the senses and keep up an indolent attention in the audience. Common sense, however, requires that there should be nothing in the scenes and machines which may appear childish and absurd. How would the wits of King Charles's time have laughed to have seen Nicolini exposed to a tempest in robes of ermine and sailing in an open boat upon a sea of pasteboard. What a field of raillery would they have been let into had they been entertained with painted dragons spitting wild fire, enchanted chariots drawn by Flanders mares, and real cascades in artificial landscapes.' The criticism is not very convincing, but it is rather valuable in informing us how the operas were placed upon the stage. They appear to have had much the same elaborateness of scenery and effects ('machines') as the Victorian pantomimes of our youth. Addison might have railed with justice at the absurdity of playing Shakespeare and other dramas in the fashionable dress of that period, with Hamlet in wig, breeches, and cocked hat, Ophelia and the Queen in hoops, and so on. This was done not only in the days of Queen Anne, but in later reigns. One thing he might have touched upon as an absurdity was the dressing up of the male characters in opera representations in what were called 'shapes.' A 'shape' was a sort of hooped petticoat reaching to the knees of the actor, held out in a circle by means of whalebone. The dress of the opera actors, both male and female, was quite a travesty of what would have been a correct dress for the part, and was as conventional as the operas themselves.

Addison, however, makes a very pertinent remark in one of his *Spectator* papers: 'There is no question but our great grandchildren will be very curious to know the reason why their forefathers used to sit together like an audience of foreigners in their own country and to hear whole plays acted before them in a tongue which they did not understand.' He complains that the producers of Italian operas conceived that nothing was capable of being well set to music that was not nonsense. He continues: 'We are transported with anything that is not English: so it be of foreign growth, let it be Italian, French, or High Dutch, it is the same thing. In short, our English music is quite rooted out, and nothing yet planted in its stead[1].'

Handel's success as a composer of operas did not

[1] See the whole interesting passage in the eighteenth number of the *Spectator*, March 21, 1711.

end with *Rinaldo*. He composed many others
which need not be catalogued here. Nor is it
necessary to mention the few Italian operas that
came as an importation from Italy between 1711
and 1728. Enough has been said in the preceding
pages to show the type of production from which
Englishmen turned when *The Beggar's Opera*
took the stage and cast ridicule on a style of
musical drama that had so much artificiality in it.
Suffice it to say that Handel's compositions
towered above all preceding work, and that much
excellent music lies hidden therein which might
with advantage be resuscitated. The following
pages must deal with the opera that Gay put
before the public and the Scotch pastoral which
influenced him in its method of arrangement.

## THE GENTLE SHEPHERD:
## THE FIRST BALLAD OPERA

WHILE the Italian opera was leading English musical taste astray, the Scottish nation held fast its own musical tradition and was not influenced by that of any other nation.

Even though the tradition that David Rizzio was the composer of certain favourite Scots songs may have been popularly believed, the people made no further effort to dive into the music of Italy for their songs. Nor were English songs greatly in favour, except several whose tunes had that particular 'snap,' or syncopation, supposed to be characteristic of Scotch music. Many of these English songs, such as might be written by Thomas D'Urfey, with tunes by English composers of the late seventeenth century, became popular in Scotland and in time were incorporated into her national song. An example of a late date —Hook's song, 'Within a mile of Edinburgh town' (1780), may be quoted, as also its earlier version, 'Twas within a furlong of Edinburgh town.'

It was Allan Ramsay, poet, wigmaker, and bookseller, who first took Scotch song seriously. Besides writing a number of songs which soon became national, and re-writing others, he collected many fragmentary remnants of the lyrics of his country, and, getting his friends to help him, he published a collection of these in *The Tea-Table Miscellany* in 1724, adding three more volumes at later dates. In 1721 he had published a collection of *Poems*, some of which had already seen the light in pamphlet form. Among these poems was a dialogue in verse, 'Patie and Roger,' followed a year or so later by 'Jenny and Meggy.' In these two pieces lies the germ of *The Gentle Shepherd*, a pastoral play published in 1725 under the patronage of Susanna, Countess of Eglington. It is doubtful whether Ramsay ever saw this pastoral play on the stage in Scotland, although Theophilus Cibber staged a version of it at Drury Lane in 1730 under the title *Patie and Peggy, or the fair Foundling.* This was a ballad opera of one act with the Scotch dialect turned into English and the whole condensed from Ramsay's pastoral.

*The Gentle Shepherd* may claim to be the first ballad opera giving the lead to Gay's *Beggar's Opera.* Ramsay's pastoral was in rhyme, with short separate songs adapted to Scotch tunes that

SCENE FROM *THE GENTLE SHEPHERD*

were well-known north of the Tweed. Versions of *The Gentle Shepherd*, besides *Patie and Peggy* mentioned above, were placed upon the English stage, generally much shortened. The most notable was one by Richard Tickell, with the music arranged and harmonised by Thomas Linley the elder. This was produced at Drury Lane in 1781.

Although Ramsay used the same method that Gay afterwards did, by employing popular tunes for his songs, *The Gentle Shepherd* is as far removed from *The Beggar's Opera* as anything can well be; yet I think that it suggested to Gay the style in which to write his opera.

*The Gentle Shepherd* bears the sub-title 'A pastoral comedy,' and this must be remembered in reading the note in Spence's *Anecdotes*, which gives the account of the conception of *The Beggar's Opera* in Pope's own words: 'Dr Swift had been observing once to Mr Gay what an odd pretty sort of thing a Newgate Pastoral might make.' In these words we have an indication that Swift and Gay had been reading or discussing *The Gentle Shepherd*, the Scotch 'Pastoral,' and Ramsay's employment of popular tunes for the songs must have given Gay a hint as to the method of introducing music.

Gay was under the patronage of the Duchess of

Queensberry, the wife of a Scottish Duke. He had probably visited Edinburgh several times, and was likely to have met Ramsay there. As is shown by the number of Scotch tunes he employed in *The Beggar's Opera,* he appears to have had not only a knowledge of Scotch music but to have admired it.

The plot of *The Gentle Shepherd* is well conceived and sufficiently dramatic. As before mentioned, the writing is entirely in rhyme, even to the description of each scene. The story deals with the loves of two shepherds, Patie and Roger, for Peggy and Jenny. Both the ladies and the men turn out to be by birth above their present station. There is a Sir William Worthy, who, having joined Montrose, has had to flee the country until the restoration of Charles II. He returns in disguise as a fortune-teller and claims Patie as his son and heir. There are other episodes to work out a rather intricate plot, and the characters include a supposed witch and a comic countryman. The piece is well written and from its first publication to the present day has always been esteemed one of Scotland's classics.

*The Gentle Shepherd* would of course be well known to Gay, Swift, Pope, and the circle that surrounded these poets. Although the Scots 'Pastoral' differs so much from the 'Newgate

Pastoral,' I thinkt here will be no great strain in coming to the conclusion that Ramsay's work suggested the 'method,' at least, in which Gay's comedy took the form of opera. It appears rather strange that no previous writer has drawn attention to the above-named similarity of treatment.

## THE BEGGAR'S OPERA:
## ITS CONCEPTION

TO continue the story of the conception of *The Beggar's Opera*, Gay seems to have been struck with Swift's suggestion of a 'Newgate Pastoral.' Pope gives an account of the writing of it in these words: 'Gay was inclined to try at such a thing, for some time, but afterwards thought it would be better to write a comedy on the same plan. This was what gave rise to *The Beggar's Opera*. He began on it and when first he mentioned it to Swift, the Doctor did not much like the project. As he carried it on, he showed what he wrote to both of us and we now and then gave a correction or a word or two of advice: but it was wholly his own writing. When it was done, neither of us thought it would succeed. We showed it to Congreve who, after reading it over, said "It would either take greatly, or be damned confoundedly." We were all at the first night of it in great uncertainty of the event; till we were very much encouraged by over-hearing the Duke of Argyle, who sat in the next box to us, say: "it will do,—it must do!—I see it in the eyes of them." This was a good while before the

first act was over and so gave us ease soon; for the
Duke (besides his own good taste) has a more
particular knack than any one now living in dis-
covering the taste of the public. He was quite
right in this, as usual. The good nature of the audience appeared stronger and stronger every act and
ended in a clamour of applause[1].'

This narrative of how the opera was conceived
and written is the most valuable record regarding
the birth of *The Beggar's Opera* which we possess.
It is especially valuable for its direct and clear
statement given by one who was intimately associated with Gay in his work. It also is most interesting in its picture of the 'first night.' What a
company in that box!—waiting with Gay for the
public's verdict on a new departure in dramatic
entertainment. Pope, Swift, perhaps Congreve,
whose works were ever welcomed as assured successes, and Gay modestly sitting in the rear, while
his friends were keenly watching the common
audience in the pit, the arbiters and best judges of
the fare set before them.

There is an interesting account of the production
of *The Beggar's Opera* in Pope's own words in

[1] The above account of the conception of the opera
was learned from Pope himself by Joseph Spence and
appears in his *Anecdotes*, 1820. Dr Johnson used the
account in his *Life of Gay* from Spence's MSS.

his notes to *The Dunciad*. Though often quoted,
it may be appropriately reproduced here:

'The vast success of it was unprecedented and
almost incredible....It was acted in London sixty-
three days uninterrupted and renewed the next
season with equal applause. It spread into all the
great towns of England, was played in many places
to the thirtieth and fortieth time, at Bath and
Bristol fifty, etc. It made its progress into Wales,
Scotland, and Ireland where it was performed
twenty-four days together; it was lastly acted in
Minorca. The fame of it was not confined to the
author only, the ladies carried about with them
the favourite songs of it in fans, and houses were
furnished with it in screens. The person who
acted Polly, till then obscure, became all at once
the favourite of the Town. Her pictures were engraved and sold in great numbers, her life written,
books of letters and verses to her published, and
pamphlets made even of her sayings and jests.

'Furthermore, it drove out of England for that
season the Italian opera, which had carried all
before it for ten years: that idol of the nobility and
people which the great critic, Mr Dennis, by the
labours and outcries of a whole life, could not
overthrow, was demolished by a single stroke of
this gentleman's pen. This remarkable period
happened in the year 1728.'

BURLESQUE OF *THE BEGGAR'S OPERA*

The lines to which Pope affixed this note run:

> While Wren with sorrow to the grave descends,
> Gay dies unpension'd, with a hundred friends.

As Pope states, *The Beggar's Opera* was acted not only in England but in many distant places where the English language was known or spoken. There is plenty of evidence that its wit and satire was appreciated in these places in the same degree as in London. In Chetwood's *History of the Stage* (1749) there is a pathetic narrative of a touring company who took *The Beggar's Opera* to Jamaica. He writes:

'I had an account from a gentleman, who was possessed of a large estate in the island, that a company in the year 1733 came there and cleared a large sum of money; where they might have made moderate fortunes, if they had not been too busy with the growth of the country. They received three hundred and seventy pistoles the first night, to *The Beggar's Opera*; but within the space of two months they buried their third Polly and two of their men. The gentlemen of the island for some time took their turns upon the stage, to keep up the diversion; but this did not hold long, for in two months more there were but one old man, a boy, and a woman of the company left. The rest died either with the country distemper or the common beverage of the place, the noble

spirit of rum punch which is generally fatal to
new-comers. The shattered remains, with upwards
of two thousand pistoles in bank, embarked for
Carolina to join another company at Charlestown,
but were cast away in the voyage. Had the company been more blessed with the virtue of sobriety
they might perhaps have lived to carry home the
liberality of those generous islanders.'

# JOHN GAY

**A**S to John Gay, the author, the following facts may be of interest. He was born at Barnstaple in 1685 and educated at the Free School there. His London life began behind the counter of a mercer's shop in the Strand, but fate directed a small legacy, sufficient to enable him to escape from shop life. He turned his attention to literature in his leisure time. In 1712 he was a domestic steward to the Duchess of Monmouth, and two years afterwards he accompanied the Earl of Clarendon to Hanover, where the Earl had been dispatched on a political mission by Queen Anne.

His disposition, his integrity, and his talents gained him esteem and elevated him from mere servitude. Caroline, then Princess of Wales, took an interest in his literary work and to her he dedicated his *Fables*, the original purpose of which was to lead by pleasant rhyme her young son, Prince William, to paths of virtue and good sense. What moral effect these charming fables had upon the Duke of Cumberland is a question of doubt when we remember his conduct at Culloden, after

which he was chiefly known as the 'Butcher' of
that miserable battlefield.

Gay looked for more than flattery from the
great people who 'took him up,' and he found
one of his best friends in the Duchess of Queensberry, the 'Kitty beautiful and young' of Prior's
poem.

The *Fables* had won him fame and, as he thought,
Court favour, but he soon found this a broken
reed, and in several passages of his opera he afterwards gave bitter expression to his conviction that
Court favour was as shallow and as false as was
proverbially alleged. He sought a place of dignity
at Court with a salary attached; but he was
offered, in 1727, the position of gentleman usher
to the youngest princess, a post he indignantly
refused. Gay's friends took up his cause warmly
—perhaps too warmly, as he appears to have lost
much of the little favour he already had. Chief
among his supporters was the warm-hearted and
impulsive Duchess of Queensberry. He had already
made many literary friends, among whom were
Pope and Swift, two powerful allies.

*The Beggar's Opera* was not his first dramatic
effort; he had long been writing for the stage, and
his first work was *The Mohocks, a tragi-comical
farce as it is acted near the Watch House in Covent
Garden.* This was an exposition of the brutality

of those men of fashion who banded themselves together for the purpose of night outrages on innocent people and general wayfarers. By these outrages they fully justified the name of the tribe of wild Indians which they assumed. The play was put forth and published anonymously in 1712, but never acted. Gay's next venture was *The Wife of Bath*, in part taken from Chaucer. This was acted at Drury Lane in 1713, but with little success. After *The Beggar's Opera* had made its author famous he tried *The Wife of Bath* at Lincoln's Inn Theatre in 1730, but it again failed to attract attention.

Next followed what Gay called 'A tragi-comipastoral farce,' entitled *The What d'ye call it*, a title as vague as Shakespeare's *As you like it*. *The What d'ye call it*, a good-natured satire upon the tragic and heavy drama then so much in vogue on the English stage, was acted at Drury Lane in 1715; its sole surviving fragment is the once popular song 'T'was when the seas were roaring.' In a three-act comedy, *Three Hours after Marriage*, acted at Drury Lane in 1717, Gay is said to have collaborated with Pope and Dr Arbuthnot. This play, in spite of its merit, met with little popular approval. Pope was so disgusted with the poor reception of the piece that he never attempted anything further in the nature of drama. The comedy, which was printed as by Gay alone, was partly a satire upon certain living personages. In 1720 Gay printed among his poems *Dione*, a pastoral, which was not acted in the author's life-time, though in 1733 it was set to music by Lampe and acted, with alterations, at the Haymarket. He also wrote *Acis and Galatea*, to which Handel set music as welcome to-day as at its birth in 1732.

Another of Gay's dramas, *The Captives*, was acted at Drury Lane in 1724 with some success. *The Beggar's Opera* followed this. Of the two dramatic productions that Gay wrote afterwards one was *Polly*, a sequel to *The Beggar's Opera*, referred to later, and the other *Achilles*, a ballad opera. This was a classic burlesque, in which Achilles is in woman's clothes throughout the piece, and songs to popular airs are used after the manner of Gay's other operas. It was acted at Covent Garden in 1733 after the death of its author. George Colman made an alteration of it in 1774 under the title *Achilles in Petticoats*, also acted at Covent Garden, but with little success.

The plot and characters in *The Beggar's Opera* are dealt with in the next chapter.

## THE PLOT AND CHARACTERS
## OF *THE BEGGAR'S OPERA*

THE principal characters are Mr Peachum and his wife (so called— but Mr Peachum asks his daughter 'Do you think your mother and I should have lived comfortably so long together if ever we had been married?'); Polly, their daughter; Lockit, the keeper of Newgate, and his daughter Lucy; Captain Macheath, a highwayman; Filch, a young man—a sort of assistant to Peachum; and a number of women of the town, rejoicing in such names as Diana Trapes, Jenny Diver, Mrs Coaxer, Dolly Trull, Mrs Slammekin, Suky Tawdry, Molly Brazen, and Betty Doxy. The male 'supers' are Macheath's gang, Jemmy Twitcher, Crook-fingered Jack, Robin of Bagshot, Matt of the Mint, Nimming Ned, and some others.

Peachum is a receiver of stolen goods and, when it suits his purpose, an informer upon any of his clients for the reward. He is associated with Lockit and shares in matters to their mutual advantage. If we are to believe Fielding's picture of Jonathan Wild, we have in him the prototype of Peachum. Throughout the whole country there must have been many Peachums. Forty pounds was the eighteenth century reward for the apprehension or impeachment of a highwayman, and hanging was a punishment for even petty stealing.

Macheath is a man of many amours and of a bright, happy disposition. He is the darling of the ladies; but the amours that concern the play are those he enjoys with Polly and Lucy. Polly is a trusting creature, thoroughly in love with the highwayman, to whom she believes she is legally married—and, as it turns out, she is right in this belief. Lucy Lockit is much of a vixen. She is equally in love with Macheath, but burns with jealous passion at his flirting with Polly. Lucy believes she is all in all to Macheath, and he has to exercise much diplomacy to satisfy each that she alone is the favoured one. With very heartfelt reason he sings:

> How happy could I be with either
> Were t'other dear charmer away,

in an interview with both ladies railing at him for his inconstancy.

The play is opened by a sort of prologue, a dialogue between a Beggar and a Player before the curtain is drawn up. The Beggar begins by saying: 'If poverty be a title to poetry I am sure

nobody can dispute mine. I own myself of the
Company of Beggars; and I make one at their
weekly festivals at St Giles's. I have a small yearly
salary for my catches, and am welcome to a dinner
there whenever I please, which is more than most
poets can say.' He goes on to explain: 'This piece
I own was originally writ for the celebrating the
marriage of James Chaunter and Moll Lay, two
most excellent ballad singers.' In this we get Gay's
excuse for employing the common street tunes
instead of specially composed music. He next has
a tilt at the Italian opera, as the Beggar continues:
'I have introduced the similes that are in all your
celebrated operas: the swallow, the moth, the
bee, the ship, the flower, etc. Besides, I have a
Prison Scene, which the ladies always reckon
charmingly pathetic.' (There were prison scenes
in several of the preceding operas.) 'As to the
parts, I have observed such nice impartiality to
our two ladies that it is impossible for either of
them to take offence.' The constant quarrels
between the ladies of the Italian opera is here
alluded to. The rivalry between Margharita de
l'Epine and Mrs Tofts is one example of this, and
others of later date might be quoted. The Beggar
goes on to say: 'I hope I may be forgiven that I
have not made my opera throughout unnatural,
like those in vogue; for I have no Recitative;

excepting this, as I have consented to have neither Prologue nor Epilogue, it must be allowed an opera in all its forms. The piece indeed hath been heretofore frequently represented by ourselves in our Great Room at St Giles's, so that I cannot too often acknowledge your charity in bringing it now on the stage.'

The overture was composed by Dr Pepusch, who was also the arranger of the melodies which Gay had selected for his songs. Running through the overture is that delightful air 'The Happy Clown' (or 'One evening having lost my way'), to which Gay adapted his song 'I'm like a skiff on the ocean tossed.' Dr Burney says that Pepusch 'furnished the wild, rude, and often vulgar melodies with basses so excellent that no sound contrapuntist will ever attempt to alter them.' Dr Burney was no doubt wise in his own generation, but richer harmonies have been fitted to what he calls 'the wild, rude, and often vulgar melodies.' His whole teaching led him to see no beauty in the charming little snatches of melody which have pleased nearly two centuries of hearers.

The first scene opens with Peachum discovered sitting at a table with a large account book before him. To the air 'An old woman clothèd in gray' he finds excuse for his nefarious dealings:

Through all the employments of life
Each neighbour abuses his brother...
The priest calls the lawyer a cheat,
The lawyer be-knaves the divine;
And the statesman because he's so great,
Thinks his trade as honest as mine.

Filch enters after the song, and here we get an insight of the power which the informer has over his victims. Filch brings word from Black Moll that 'her trial comes on in the afternoon and she hopes you will order matters so as to bring her off.' Peachum tells Filch that he may assure her—'as the wench is very active and industrious you may satisfy her that I'll soften the evidence.' Tom Gagg is denounced as a 'lazy dog'—'when I took him the time before, I told him what he would come to if he did not mend his hand. This is death without reprieve. I may venture to book him (writes) "For Tom Gagg forty pounds."' The message sent to Betty Sly is that he will save her from transportation 'for I can get more by her staying in England. She may,' he continues, 'live a twelvemonth longer.' And so forth in this strain with a number of criminals.

That this method of the receiver and informer is an accurate picture of the corrupt system in vogue in the early part of the eighteenth century there is enough evidence to show. Filch is sent off to Newgate to 'let my friends know what I intend; for I love to make them easy one way or the other,' says Peachum.

He now reviews the work done by each of the criminals under his thumb. Crook-fingered Jack has been industrious, having to his credit a lengthy list of articles, while Slippery Sam goes off the next session, as he has 'the impudence to have views of following his trade as a tailor, which he calls an honest employment.' Mrs Peachum enters at the mention of Bob Booty and hopes 'nothing bad hath betided him,' as he is a favourite customer of hers and gave her a ring. Peachum replies that he is too fond of women and that 'the ladies will hang him for the reward, and there's forty pound lost to us for ever.'

All this satire, bitter though it be, is sufficiently true in fact to show the evils of tempting men to steal and then gaining money by betraying them. There can be no doubt that numbers of men and the women of the town made this a profitable trade. Strange it is that eighteenth-century citizens who lived while this was going on day by day could find nothing in *The Beggar's Opera* to condemn save what they imagined to be the glorification of a highwayman, and missed the whole point as to the evils which Gay so fearlessly and so vigorously pointed out. In all the criticism that has been levelled at the piece every writer has ignored this obvious lesson and could find no other motive for the opera save political satire or a ridicule of the Italian opera.

The conversation between Mrs Peachum and her husband drifts in the direction of Polly and of her fondness for Captain Macheath. Peachum becomes alarmed at the idea of a marriage between the Captain and his daughter, chiefly because of the danger that Macheath might hang his father-in-law by his evidence. By questioning Filch Mrs Peachum discovers that Polly is duly married to Macheath. Polly now enters and is reproached by both father and mother for this indiscretion. There is a terrible to-do and much discussion by father and mother as to the best to be done for their interest and safety. It is decided that Macheath must hang to keep the reward in the family. At this Polly kneels before father and mother in turn and pleads for his life to the beautiful old ballad air belonging to *The Children in the Wood.*

> Oh ponder well, be not severe,
> So save a wretched wife;
> For on the rope that hangs my dear
> Depends poor Polly's life.

It is said that the fate of the opera was undecided until this passage, but that the beautiful air, the plaintive words, and the pathetic picture of Polly kneeling aroused the enthusiasm of the audience and that the opera went safely from this point.

Mrs Peachum tells Polly: 'Your duty to your parents, hussy, obliges you to hang him. What would many a wife give for such an opportunity!... Away, hussy, hang your husband and be dutiful.'

Polly alone pictures to herself the execution of her loved husband—'Methinks I see him already in the cart, sweeter and more lovely than the nosegay in his hand—I hear the crowd extolling his resolution and intrepidity. What volleys of sighs are sent from the windows of Holborn that so comely a youth should be brought to disgrace! I see him at the tree. The whole circle are in tears, even butchers weep. Jack Ketch himself hesitates to perform his duty and would be glad to lose his fee by a reprieve.'

She goes to tell him of his danger. Follows a scene between Polly and Macheath in which, after much protestation, the highwayman takes leave of Polly. This concludes the first act of the original version of the play.

The next act rises on a tavern near Newgate. Here are assembled Macheath's gang—Jemmy Twitcher, Crook-fingered Jack, Robin of Bagshot, and the rest. They are drinking, and Ben Budge, who has just returned from transportation, is enquiring after one of the gang, who, it appears, has had an 'accident,' meaning that he has paid for his misdeeds with his life. There is much thieves' philosophy talked and finally they join in a drinking song, 'Fill every glass,' to a rich French 'round.' At its conclusion Macheath enters and tells the gang that he must fly for his life, but that he will continue to meet them at their private quarters at Moorfields.

Now comes a chorus of the gang adapted to the march in Handel's opera, *Rinaldo*.

> Let us take the road.
> Hark! I hear the sound of coaches!
> The hour of attack approaches,
> To your arms, brave boys, and load.
>
> See the ball I hold!
> Let the chymists toil like asses,
> Our fire their fire surpasses
> And turns all our lead to gold.

The gang, 'ranged in front of the stage, load their pistols, and stick them under their girdles; then go off, singing the first part in chorus.'

Macheath, now alone, soliloquises and declares that he loves the sex, 'and a man who loves money might as well be contented with one guinea as I with one woman.' He now sings one of the most popular of the airs:

> If the heart of a man is deprest with cares,
> The mist is dispelled when a woman appears, etc.

The tune, 'Would you have a young virgin of

fifteen years,' figured in many a Victorian drawing room as the bowing figure in the Lancers. He now asks the tavern drawer if the porter has gone for all the ladies, 'according to my directions.' The drawer expects the porter back every minute, 'but you know, sir, you sent him as far as Hockley in the Hole for three of the ladies, for one in Vinegar Yard, and for the rest of them somewhere about Lewkner's Lane. Sure some of them are below, for I hear the bar bell; as they come I will show them up.' And so now enters a bevy of ladies of the town, among whom are Mrs Coaxer, Dolly Trull, Mrs Vixen, Betty Doxy, Jenny Diver, Mrs Slammekin, and some others equally blessed with suggestive names. Macheath welcomes each as they enter with well chosen compliments and advice. Then enters an opportune harper, who, at the highwayman's request plays 'the French tune that Mrs Slammekin was so fond of.' A French cotillon is danced 'A la ronde in the French manner,' and near the end of it all the ladies and Macheath sing to the air:

> Youth's the season made for joys,
> 　Love is then our duty;
> She alone who that employs
> 　Well deserves her beauty.
> 　　Let's be gay
> 　　While we may,
> Beauty's a flower despised in decay, etc.

After this pretty dance and song Macheath bids the ladies take their places for wine—'If any of the ladies choose gin, I hope they will be so free to call for it.' The ladies, however, are scant of gratitude; for after some pleasant conversation one lady playfully takes one pistol from him, while another disarms him of the other. Jenny Diver then says 'I must and will have a kiss to give my wine a zest,' and so, while he is being embraced by two of the ladies, they make signs to Peachum and a constable, who secure him as prisoner. As he is led off Peachum remarks: 'Ladies, I'll take care the reckoning shall be discharged.' The women now quarrel as to how the reward is to be shared.

I will now reiterate my former statement, that so far there is nothing overdrawn in this picture of life among the class it represents. That thieves have been betrayed by receivers of stolen goods and by their doxies is no new thing, either in fiction or in real life, and I must again say that those who have condemned *The Beggar's Opera* for its supposed immorality have been utterly blind to the moral it endeavoured, unsuccessfully, it must be granted, to teach. There is nothing said as to the immorality of the pictures and engravings by William Hogarth. He is accepted as a moralist and a sincere teacher, which without doubt he certainly was, though the scenes he has

depicted are in many cases far more disgusting
than any scene in Gay's opera. Hogarth had the
highest sympathy with the opera and appears to
have been the one man in that age who understood its mission. He disregarded its political satire
and its tilting at the absurdities of the Italian opera.
These were minor matters to men who thought
as broadly as Hogarth. Had Hogarth not been a
painter he would have written a Beggar's Opera
of far greater fierceness than gentle John Gay.

The next scene after Macheath's arrest is laid
in Newgate. Here he is being fettered by Lockit
and has to pay for a lighter set of irons than the
keeper of Newgate (for the purpose of extorting
money) threatened him with. This particular
imposition and form of cruelty is also a true record
of the sufferings the imprisoned had to endure
unless they could heavily bribe the jailer. Macheath, left alone fettered in the cell, bewails his
lot. 'To what a woeful plight have I brought
myself! Here must I (all day long till I am hanged)
be confined to hear the reproaches of a wench
who lays her ruin at my door. I am in the custody
of her father, and, to be sure, if he knows of the
matter I shall have a fine time on't between this
and my execution....But here comes Lucy, and I
cannot get from her; would I were deaf.'

Macheath is right in his anticipation. Lucy

enters and rails at him in no small measure. She betrays her jealousy of Polly Peachum and vows that she could tear her eyes out. 'Are you not married to her, you brute?' she queries. He denies it. 'The wench gives it out only to vex thee' is his excuse. He makes many promises, and as Lucy begins to soften under that of marriage the scene closes.

Still in Newgate, we next have an interview between Peachum and Lockit; they are sharing their spoils with an account-book in front of them. Lockit says: 'In this last affair, brother Peachum, we are agreed. You have consented to go halves in Macheath.' Peachum replies: 'We shall never fall out about an execution—but as to that article, pray how stands our last year's account?' Lockit assures his colleague that he will find it all clearly stated. Peachum complains of the Government's delay in paying rewards for information. 'Can it be expected,' he asks, 'that we would hang our acquaintance for nothing when our betters will hardly save theirs without being paid for it? Unless the people in employment pay better, I promise them for the future I shall let other rogues live besides their own.' Lockit remarks: 'Perhaps, brother, they are afraid these matters may be carried too far. We are treated too by them with contempt, as if our profession were not reputable.' Now begins a quarrel between these

two worthies. Peachum draws attention to the case
of Ned Clincher: 'Sure, brother Lockit, there was
a little unfair proceeding in Ned's case; for he told
me in the condemned hold that for value received
you had promised him a session or two longer
without molestation.' Lockit waxes indignant.
'Mr Peachum,' he cries, 'this is the first time my
honour was ever called in question.' Peachum, virtuous, replies: 'Business is at an end if once we act
dishonourably.' Lockit resents the imputation and
Peachum still further charges him with defrauding
Mrs Coaxer of her information money for the
apprehending of Curl-pated Hugh. He continues:
'We must punctually pay our spies or we shall
have no information.' Lockit bursts out: 'Is this
language to me, sirrah, who have saved you from
the gallows?' They seize each other by the collar,
Peachum saying, 'If I am hanged, it shall be for
ridding the world of an arrant rascal.' And so the
quarrel goes on, till it occurs to them that it is not
policy to fall out with one another. Peachum cries:
'Brother, brother, we are both in the wrong. We
shall be both losers in the dispute, for you know we
have it in our power to hang each other. You
should not be so passionate.' 'Nor you so pro-
voking,' replies Lockit, and so the altercation ends.

Lucy now enters and greets her father. She is
scolded for grieving over the coming fate of her

lover Macheath. Lockit uses the same reasoning that Peachum used to his daughter, concluding, 'Look ye, Lucy, there is no saving him, so I think you must even do like other widows—buy yourself weeds and be cheerful...So make yourself as easy as you can by getting all you can from him.'

Lucy then has an interview with Macheath. The highwayman suggests that a bribe of twenty pounds might lead to his escape. Lucy assures him that 'what love or money can do shall be done.' At this moment Polly rushes into the scene crying for her 'dear husband,' to the consternation of Macheath, who has vowed to Lucy that he is not married to Polly.

In this scene occurs that pretty song, once so popular, sung by Polly:

> Cease your funning;
> Force or cunning
> Never shall my heart trepan.
> All these sallies
> Are but malice
> To seduce my constant man, etc.

This is followed by the dialogue song sung by Lucy and Polly:

> Why how now, Madam Flirt?
> If you thus must chatter
> And are for flinging dirt,
>    Let's try who best can spatter,
>       Madam Flirt!

Polly replies:

> Why how now, saucy jade?
> Sure the wench is tipsy!
> How can you see me made
>     The scoff of such a gipsy?
>         Saucy jade!

Peachum comes in and drags Polly away. Macheath, left alone with Lucy, assures her that Polly has no claim on him; Lucy believes him. She steals the keys and effects his release.

After a short scene in a gaming house, into which Macheath has ventured, we find Lockit and Peachum discussing the details of the stolen goods in which they have shares. To them enters Diana Trapes, who incidentally gives the whereabouts of Macheath. They promise her a reward for this information, and at a later scene in the play he is recaptured and brought again to Newgate.

Meanwhile there is an interview between Lucy and Polly. Lucy disguises her hatred of Polly and presses upon her a glass of poisoned wine. Polly suspects Lucy of some mischief and does not drink from the glass, dropping it as she sees Macheath brought in under custody. Lucy and Polly fall on their knees to their respective fathers and beg for his life. This is a scene of which Hogarth painted one or more pictures. The two fathers

SCENE FROM *THE BEGGAR'S OPERA*

are obdurate, and Macheath is led off to the Old
Bailey for his trial. Polly bids Filch follow and
bring her a report of his behaviour at his trial.
Music is heard, and when Lucy and Polly have
retired there is a dance of prisoners in chains, as
their trials are put off until next session.

The following scene shows Macheath after his
sentence in the Condemned Hold. He is seated at
a table with a bottle of wine and a glass before
him. He sings a curious song, set to fragments of
ten songs, forming a sort of medley. It concludes
with:

> Since laws were made for every degree,
> To curb vice in others as well as me,
> I wonder we hav'nt better company
>     Upon Tyburn Tree.

> But gold from law can take out the sting;
> And if rich men, like us, were to swing,
> T'would thin the land such numbers to string
>     Upon Tyburn Tree.

This is set to a very corrupt version of the sixteenth century air, 'Greensleeves.'

Some of the gang now enter and condole with
Macheath on his impending fate.

He tells them that 'Peachum and Lockit...are
infamous scoundrels. Their lives are as much in
your power as yours are in theirs. Remember your
dying friend! 'Tis my last request. Bring those

villains to the gallows before you—and I am satisfied.'

In this little passage Gay points the whole moral of the piece. It is not, as so many people have thought, a glorification of the lives of thieves and a highwayman, but an exposure of the vile system which allowed such men as Lockit and Peachum to exist, to make criminals for their benefit, and to betray them to justice after they have served this turn, for the reward.

Polly and Lucy now arrive to take leave of their lover. Macheath advises them to ship themselves off to the West Indies, 'where you'll have a fair chance of getting a husband apiece, or, by good luck, two or three, as you like best.'

In the midst of this scene the jailer announces 'Four women more, captain, with a child apiece.' 'What!' cries Macheath, 'four wives more—this is too much; here, tell the Sheriff's officers I am ready.' Exit guarded.

The Player and the Beggar now enter. The Player expostulates with the Beggar. He says: 'But, honest friend, I hope you don't intend that Macheath shall be really executed.' The Beggar replies: 'Most certainly, sir. To make the piece perfect, I was for doing strict poetical justice. Macheath is to be hanged; and for the other personages of the drama, the audience must have supposed they were all either hanged or transported.' The Player cries: 'Why then, friend, this is a downright deep tragedy. The catastrophe is manifestly wrong, for an opera must end happily.' 'Your objection, sir,' says the Beggar, 'is very just, and is easily removed; for you must allow that in this kind of drama 'tis no matter how absurdly things are brought about. So—you rabble, there—run and cry a reprieve!—let the prisoner be brought back to his wives in triumph.' The Player admits 'all this we must do, to comply with the taste of the town.'

The Beggar now shows really what was in Gay's mind when he wrote the play. He continues: 'Through the whole piece you may observe such a similitude of manners in high and low life that it is difficult to determine whether (in the fashionable vices) the fine gentlemen imitate the gentlemen of the road, or the gentlemen of the road the fine gentlemen. Had the play remained as I at first intended, it would have carried a most excellent moral. T'would have shown that the lower sort of people have their vices in a degree as well as the rich, and that they are punished for them.'

Macheath is brought on the stage again and the play concludes with a dance, Macheath singing a song to the old tune, 'Lumps of Pudding,' after confessing that he has legally married Polly. The

use of the above-named air caused it to be said
that the Italian opera had been driven off the
stage by 'lumps of pudding.'

Such, then, is an epitome of *The Beggar's Opera*,
one of the brightest, wittiest dramas of the
eighteenth century. It has had more invective
hurled at it during the two centuries of its career
than any of the many questionable comedies that
followed or were contemporary with it. What
political satire there was in it is of little weight
to-day. Surely everybody of that age knew that
politics were in a corrupt state and that each
statesman used the country and the country's
purse for his own advantage; and, what was still
more to be deplored, that art and literature for a
long time were under the ban or the protection of
one political party or another, and that the arts
were not judged entirely upon their own intrinsic
merits but were condemned or praised as they
came from the camp of a friend or an enemy. It
is quite obvious to modern eyes that *The Beggar's
Opera* was not wholly a political satire, as has
been stated; also that it was not wholly a satire
upon the Italian opera, though it levelled a shaft
at its absurdities. The active motive of the piece
was decidedly an exposure of the system which
produced and fostered such rascals as Peachum
and Lockit.

There are oft-repeated statements to the effect that Gay was indebted to several of his friends for certain songs in the opera. For example, Sir Walter Scott writes: 'About this time Swift is supposed to have supplied Gay with the two celebrated songs, afterwards ingrafted in *The Beggar's Opera*, beginning "Through all the employments of life," and "Since laws were made for every degree."' And again in Macklin's *Memoirs* (1804), the statement is made, from the information of the Dowager Lady Townshend, that 'The modes of the court' was written by Lord Chesterfield, 'Virgins are like the fair flower' by Sir Charles Hanbury Williams, 'When you censure the age' by Swift, and 'Gamesters and lawyers are jugglers alike' by Mr Fortescue, the Master of the Rolls.

That Gay was indebted for any help in his piece (save for very slight suggestions from Swift and Pope) there is little real evidence to show. The different statements that he accepted songs written by others may be dismissed with very little ceremony.

## THE MUSIC OF *THE BEGGAR'S OPERA* AND ITS SOURCES

IN the prologue of the Beggar and Player Gay tells us that the opera was written to celebrate 'the marriage of James Chaunter and Moll Lay, two most excellent ballad singers.' Here, then, was the motive to use the common street tunes with which everybody was then familiar, interspersed with a few from more remote sources, chiefly the French airs.

At this period Thomas Cross, a music engraver, was flooding the town with roughly engraved or etched songs, having the music and printed on half sheets of paper. It had been usual, before his advent, to put forth songs in collections of twenty, thirty, or more, either the composition of one musician or by a number of musicians. Such are the publications of John and Henry Playford under such titles as *The Treasury of Musick, The Banquet of Musick,* and similar nomenclature. Dr John Blow bewails the new method in his *Amphion Anglicus* (1700) thus:

Music of many parts hath now no force.
Whole reams of single songs become our curse....
While at the shops we daily dangling view
False concords by Tom Cross engraven true.

The songs which Cross so industriously engraved
were mainly of the more popular class sung at the
theatres, etc. Many were by Tom D'Urfey.
When D'Urfey issued his various editions of *Wit
and Mirth, or Pills to Purge Melancholy*, he reproduced many of these songs in the six volumes that
he ultimately published—the last was dated 1720,
the previous five volumes bearing the date 1719.
It is quite certain that Gay must have possessed a
set of these books, and, as I shall endeavour to
show, to them he turned for many of the airs
employed in the opera. Gay also inclined to the
songs of Scotland, and we find that the bulk of
those selected are to be found in William Thomson's *Orpheus Caledonius*, a folio volume con-
taining fifty Scotch songs, for the first time collected together. The book is not dated, but its
entry in Stationers' Hall on January 5th, 1725–26,
establishes the date of its issue. It is probable that
Gay had a copy of this work, perhaps presented
by his patroness the Duchess of Queensberry,
who, with her husband, was a subscriber for three
copies. Thomson was a music master, who, perhaps, instructed the family of Caroline, Princess

of Wales, afterwards Queen Consort. Thomson dedicates his book to her, and his subscription list appears to contain the names of nearly all the English and Scottish nobility and persons of note.

Another source of Gay's selected tunes must have been an edition of Playford's *Dancing Master*, which after its first appearance in 1650 ran through seventeen or eighteen editions down to the year 1728.

Dr Pepusch, a German musician, scholarly and dry, was chosen to put basses to the airs and to compose an overture. It is doubtful whether he had any hand in the selection of the tunes. He does not appear to have been able to speak very good English, and it is noticeable that, while there are a number of French tunes employed, there are none of German origin, if we exclude Handel's march from *Rinaldo*. Surely Pepusch, seeing popular airs were in request, would have introduced one or more German folk songs into the opera if he had the duty of finding simple melodies for Gay's verses.

As there are several French tunes interspersed, Gay had no doubt access to a French collection, which I have not yet been able to identify; or else they have been noted down from songs sung by some of his friends.

The following will give some information re-

garding the English and Scottish tunes employed
in the opera:—

I      *Through all the employments of life*
Air: 'An old woman clothèd in gray.' (This is
the opening tune to which Peachum sings his
excuse for his career.) The original song begins:

> An old woman clothèd in gray
> Whose daughter was charming and young,
> But chanced to be once led astray
> By Roger's false flattering tongue.

This is on early eighteenth-century music sheets.
In *The Dancing Master* it is named 'Unconstant
Roger,' after the 'Roger' of the song.

II      *'Tis woman that seduces all mankind*
Air: 'The bonny grey-ey'd morn.' An Anglo-
Scotch song, the air of which is believed to be by
Jeremiah Clark. It is in vol. III of *Pills* (1719)
and on half-sheet music.

III      *If any wench Venus's girdle wears*
Air: 'Cold and Raw.' Another Anglo-Scotch
song, of which there are several versions. In vol.
III of *Pills* (1719) it is called 'The Farmer's
Daughter.' The anecdote given by Hawkins re-
lating to Queen Mary asking Mrs Arabella
Hunt, in Purcell's presence, if she could not sing
'Cold and Raw,' and Purcell introducing the air
into the bass of a birthday ode, is well-known.

IV     *If love the virgin's heart invade*

Air: 'Why is your faithful slave disdained?' This occurs in an indifferent form in *Pills*, vol. III (1719). The set in *The Beggar's Opera* is much finer.

V     *A maid is like the golden ore*

Air: 'Of all the simple things we do.' This is in vol. I of *Pills* (1719) and elsewhere. It is frequently named 'Marriage, or the Mouse Trap.' Under the title 'Old Hob, or the Mouse Trap,' the tune is in the second volume of *The Dancing Master* (1719).

VI     *Virgins are like the fair flower*

Air: 'What shall I do to show how much I love her?' This is by Henry Purcell, from his *History of Dioclesian*. It is also in *Pills*, vol. IV.

VII     *Our Polly is a sad slut*

Air: 'Oh London is a fine town.' An early and very popular air, set to a merry song. It is in *Pills*, vol. V, and on half-sheet music.

VIII     *Can love be controlled by advice*

Air: 'Grim king of the ghosts.' The air is used for N. Rowe's song 'Colin's Complaint' and other songs. *Pills*, vol. VI (1720).

IX   *Oh Polly, you might have toyed and kissed*
Air: 'Oh Jenny, oh Jenny, where hast thou
been?' The song is in *Pills*, vol. i. It is also known
as 'The Willoughby Whim,' and as 'May Fair.'
To-day every school child knows the air as
'Golden slumbers kiss your eyes.'

X        *I like a ship in storms was tost*
Air: 'Thomas, I cannot.' An early tune found
among music for the Virginals. A later printed
copy, as 'Thomas you cannot,' occurs in *The
Dancing Master* (1670), and elsewhere. In Scotch
collections it is set to 'My mither says I mauna.'

XI        *A fox may steal your hens, sir*
Air: 'A soldier and a sailor.' In *Pills*, vol. iii.

XII       *Oh ponder well, be not severe*
Air: 'Now ponder well.' A beautiful old ballad
air used for 'The Children in the Wood.' The
tune, set to other words was, perhaps, first printed
in *Pills* (1709).

XIII   *The turtle thus with plaintive crying*
Air: 'Le printemps rappelle aux armes.' Not traced.

XIV           *Pretty Polly, say*
Air: 'Pretty Parrot, say.' Said to be translated
from the French. It is on early half-sheet music,
as by Mr Freeman.

XV *My heart was so free*
Air: 'Pray, fair one, be kind.' Not traced.

XVI *Were I laid on Greenland's coast*
Air: 'Over the hills and far away.' A Scottish air
used in the play *The Recruiting Officer* (1706). It
is in *Pills* (1709), and many sets of verses have
been adapted to it. One early Scottish version is:
'The wind has blawn my plaid away.'

XVII *Oh what pain it is to part*
Air: 'Gin thou wert mine awn thing.' As 'a
Scotch song' it is on half-sheet music and under
the better known title, 'An thou were my ain
thing,' in *Orpheus Caledonius* (1725–6).

XVIII *The miser thus a shilling sees*
Air: 'O the broom,' also in *Orpheus Caledonius*.

XIX *Fill every glass, for wine inspires us*
Air: 'Fill every glass,' originally a French song
and probably a French tune. It is in *Pills*, vol. 1
(1719), as 'A drinking song in praise of our
three fam'd generals,' in French with an English
translation.

XX *Let us take the road*
Air: March in *Rinaldo*. This fine tune is from
Handel's opera (1711).

XXI    *If the heart of a man is deprest*
         *with cares*

Air: 'Would you have a young virgin of fifteen years.' An early air called 'Poor Robin's Maggot.' The song and air above-named are in *Pills*, vol. I.

XXII   *Youth's the season made for joys*

Air: 'Cotillon.' This is a French cotillon called 'Zoney's Rant,' in the third volume of *The Dancing Master* (*circ.* 1726).

XXIII   *Before the barn door crowing*

Air: 'All in a misty morning.' Under the title of 'The Wiltshire Wedding' this is in *Pills*, vol. IV. An earlier name for the tune is 'The Fryar and the nun,' in *The Dancing Master*, 1650 and later editions.

XXIV    *The gamesters and lawyers*

Air: 'When once I lay.' The proper title for this air is 'The King's Delight.' It is in *Musick's Handmaid* (1678), and other of Playford's publications.

XXV  *At the tree I shall suffer with pleasure*

Air: 'When first I laid siege to my Chloris.' The words of the original song are by Sir Charles Sedley. The air is in *Pills*, vol. VI (1720).

**XXVI**    *Man may escape from rope and gun*
Air: 'Courtiers, courtiers, think it no harm.' The
song is on early half-sheet music.

**XXVII**    *Thus when a good housewife sees a rat*
Air: 'A lovely lass to a friar came.' On early
half-sheet music. The song and air are in Watts'
*Musical Miscellany* (1731).

**XXVIII**    *How cruel are the traitors*
Air: ''Twas when the sea was roaring.' The
original song is from Gay's play *The What d'ye
call it*. The music is on half-sheets.

**XXIX**    *The first time at the looking glass*
Air: 'The sun had loosed his weary teams.' This
belongs to a song called 'The Winchester Christening,' set to the country dance called 'The
Hemp Dresser.' 'The Winchester Christening' is
in *A Third Collection of New Song, the words by
Mr D'Urfey* (1685), and other places. In Scotland
the tune is set to 'The Deil's awa wi the excise-
man.' 'The Hemp Dresser' is in *The Dancing
Master* (1650 and later editions).

**XXX**    *When you censure the age*
Air: 'How happy are we who from thinking are
free.' Composed by John Barrett and 'Sung and
acted by Mr Pack.'

**XXXI**  *Is then his fate decreed, sir?*

Air: 'Of a noble race was Shenkin.' This song appears in D'Urfey's play *The Richmond Heiress* (1693). See also *Pills*, vols. II and IV. The tune has been claimed as Welsh, but the music to the play was by John Eccles and Henry Purcell. It is probably by one or the other.

**XXXII**  *You'll think e'er many days ensue*

(No title given to air.) The air was the stage traditional tune for Ophelia's song, 'How should I your true love know.'

**XXXIII**  *If you at an office solicit your due*

Air: 'London Ladies.' The tune is in *The Dancing Master*, and different editions of *Pills*. The song begins:

> Ladies of London both wealthy and fair,
> Whom every town fop is pursuing.

**XXXIV**  *Thus when the swallow, seeking prey*

Air: 'All in the downs.' This is an air to Gay's song, 'Black-ey'd Susan.' It is by P. G. Sandoni, a harpsichord maker and husband of the singer Cuzzoni. This is the least known of the airs, of which there were several, to Gay's earlier song.

**XXXV**  *How happy could I be with either*

Air: 'Have you heard of a frolicsome ditty?' The air was also called 'The Rant.' It is a seventeenth-century air to which a number of songs were sung. The song indicated in *The Beggar's Opera* is 'Give an ear to a frolicsome ditty,' and describes the adventures of a rake through the town. Another title for the tune is 'The City Ramble.'

### XXXVI     *I'm bubbled*

Air: 'Irish Trot.' Probably an alternative tune to 'The Hide Park Frolic,' in *Pills*, vol. IV, p. 138.

### XXXVII     *Cease your funning*

(No title to air.) The tune is a late seventeenth-century air, found on half-sheet music with the song 'Constant Billy.' The original song begins:

> When the hills and lofty mountains
> And the vales were hid in snow.

It is also called 'Lofty Mountains.' The air appears as 'Constant Billy' in the third volume of *The Dancing Master*.

### XXXVIII     *Why how now, Madam Flirt*

Air: 'Gossip Joan.' The song 'Good morrow, Gossip Joan' is late seventeenth-century. It is in *Pills*, vol. IV, and on half-sheet music.

### XXXIX     *No power on earth can e'er divide*

Air: 'Irish Howl.' The tune is in the third volume of *The Dancing Master* (*circ.* 1726).

XL        *I like the fox shall grieve*

Air: 'The lass of Patie's Mill.' The song is by Ramsay, and the air is in *Orpheus Caledonius* (1725–6), etc. It is also found under the title 'Peggy's Mill.'

XLI      *When young at the bar you first taught me to score*

Air: 'If love's a sweet passion, how can it torment?' The air is by Henry Purcell and is used in his *Fairy Queen*. It is printed in vol. III of *Pills* and on half sheets. There was a later setting of the song by Joseph Baildon.

XLII      *My love is all madness and folly*

Air: 'South Sea Ballad.' A tune to one of the many ballads contemporary with the South Sea Bubble.

XLIII      *Thus gamesters united in friendship are found*

Air: 'Packington's Pound.' This early air is named after Sir John Packington. It is in print in 1596, and occurs in the Fitzwilliam Virginal Manuscript, and was a popular tune through several centuries, adapted to different songs.

XLIV      *The modes of the Court so common are grown*

Air: 'Lillibulero,' the well-known party tune which, on the authority of Bishop Burnet, so helped the cause of William of Orange against James II. It was a quick step to a military march, and was printed in 1686, arranged by Henry Purcell.

## XLV    *What gudgeons are we men*

Air: 'Down in the North Country.' A popular seventeenth-century tune under various names and with various songs. The particular song indicated in *The Beggar's Opera* is 'The Farmer's daughter of merry Wakefield.'

## XLVI    *In the days of my youth*

Air: 'A shepherd kept sheep.' The song is in *Pills*, vol. v, p. 35.

## XLVII    *I'm like a skiff on the ocean tossed*

Air: 'One evening, having lost my way.' The title for this song is 'The Happy Clown'; another title is 'Walpole.' It is in the second volume of *The Dancing Master* (1718), etc.

## XLVIII    *When a wife's in her pout*

Air: 'Now, Roger, I'll tell thee because thou'rt my son.' A traditional version of this song begins:

> And now my dear Robin, since thou art my son,
> I'll give you good counsel in life,
> Go haste thee away and make no delay
> And I'll warrant I'll get thee a wife.

XLIX    *A curse attends that woman's love*

Air: 'Bessy Bell.' A Scotch tune, to be found in *Orpheus Caledonius* and elsewhere.

L       *Among the men coquets we find*

Air: 'Would fate to me Belinda give.' A song by John Wilford, *circ.* 1710.

LI       *Come, sweet lass*

Air: 'Come sweet lass, this bonny weather.' The tune is called 'Greenwich Park' in the second part of *The Dancing Master* (1698). The song is in *Pills*, vol. 1 (1719).

LII    *Hither, dear husband, turn your eyes*

Air: 'The last time I went o'er the moor.' The Scotch song is in *Orpheus Caledonius* (1725–6). It is an early Scottish tune.

LIII    *Which way shall I turn me*

Air: 'Tom Tinker's my true love.' A very coarse song. It occurs in *Pills*, vol. vi (1720). Another tune, also called 'Tom Tinker,' is to be found in *The Dancing Master* (1665).

LIV    *When my hero in court appears*

Air: 'I am a poor shepherd undone.' As 'The distressed shepherd' the song is in *Pills*, vol. vi (1720). An earlier name for the tune is 'Hey ho, my honey.'

LV     *When he holds up his hand*
Air: 'Ianthe the lovely.' The air is by John Barrett.

LVI     *The charge is prepared*
Air: 'Bonny Dundee.' A Scottish air (not the modern 'Bonnets of Bonny Dundee') in *Orpheus Caledonius* (1725–6) and elsewhere.

LVII Macheath sings fragments of ten songs in a medley. The old airs are. 'Happy Groves,' by John Barrett; 'Of all the girls that are so smart,' Carey's tune to his 'Sally in our alley'; 'Britons strike home,' by Purcell in *Bonduca*; 'Chevy Chase'; 'To old Simon the King,' one of the airs beloved by Squire Western in 'Tom Jones'—it is in print in 1652; 'Joy to great Cæsar'—the air is 'Farinels Ground,' and the song, called 'The King's Health,' in *Pills*, vol. II (1719); 'There was an old woman'—the air is in *The Dancing Master* (1703) as 'Puddings and Pies'; 'Did you ever hear of a gallant sailor?'—the song and tune is in *Pills*, vol. III (1707): 'Why are mine eyes still flowing,' in *Pills*, vol. II (1719); 'Greensleeves,' a very corrupt eighteenth-century version of the Elizabethan tune—a number of songs set to the late version of the air are in *Pills*.

LVIII     *Would I might be hanged*
Air: 'All you that must take a leap in the dark.' The song, with the air, is on half-sheet music as

*A hymn upon the execution of two criminals by Mr Ramondon.*

LIX    *Thus I stand like the Turk with his doxies around*

Air: 'Lumps of pudding.' The tune is in *The Dancing Master* (1703), and the song with the air is in *Pills*, vol. VI (1720). It is known in Scotland as associated with Burns's song, 'Contented wi' little.'

The following song is not at present in the first edition of the opera, but occurs in the third and other editions:

*Ourselves, like the great, to secure a retreat*

Air: 'A cobler there was.' The song is a humorous production called 'The cobler's end.' It is in Watts' *Musical Miscellany* (1731). The tune is a 'Derry down' air, seventeenth-century, and has been used for a number of songs, early and late.

## POLLY: THE SEQUEL TO
## THE BEGGAR'S OPERA

T is obvious that Gay, having made such a success of *The Beggar's Opera*, should wish for a further triumph on the same lines. Polly Peachum had so pleased the town with her simplicity and charm that he decided she should again figure as the heroine. There is a slight hint in *The Beggar's Opera* that Gay intended to place the scene of this next venture in the West Indies, for Macheath in the last scene advises Polly and Lucy to ship themselves off to the West Indies, where, he says, 'you'll have a fair chance of getting a husband apiece, or, by good luck, two or three, as you like best.'

Unfortunately Gay, or his political friends, had aroused some ill-feeling in the opposite camp, a political party which was then in power. It was whispered that Gay was the author of certain pamphlets which were displeasing—whether he was so or not is not quite clear, but at any rate the enemy was only too anxious to find a rope to hang their dog, and Gay's new opera came to an untimely end. Rehearsals were in full progress and

# POLLY:

## AN

# OPERA.

## BEING THE

## SECOND PART

### OF THE

## *BEGGAR's OPERA.*

---

Written by Mr. *GAY.*

---

*Rarò antecedentem fceleftum*
*Deferuit pede pœna claudo.*  Hor.

---

TITLE-PAGE OF *POLLY*

everything appeared to be going on swimmingly. Gay left the libretto with the Lord Chamberlain, who, without assigning any reason, prohibited the play from being performed. As a matter of fact it never was performed in Gay's life-time, and probably this was no misfortune to the reputation which Gay had won by *The Beggar's Opera.* The Duchess of Queensberry, always an enthusiastic patron of Gay, exerted herself towards a subscription, and it is said that the profit from the sale of copies was far greater than what he might have received had the opera been performed.

The new opera, *Polly,* lacks all the wit and brilliancy that has kept *The Beggar's Opera* alive for so many generations. The plot is absurd, the dialogue weak and poor, without any sparkle. The characters do not enlist either liking or dislike, they are merely paste-board.

There is a little fun and satire in the 'Introduction' or prologue. The Poet and the Player meet. The Poet expresses his reluctance to give the theatre a sequel: 'Contrary to my opinion I bring "Polly" once again upon the stage....My dependence, like a tricking bookseller's, is that the kind reception the first part met with will carry off the second.' Sundry players enter. One tells that it is impossible to perform the opera to-night—'The tenor...flung his clean lambskin

gloves into the fire; he swears that in his whole
life he never did sing, would sing, or could sing
but in true kid.' Signora Crotchetta is in a fury
because her character is 'so low.' The Player
reminds her that nine or ten years ago she appeared
in a character little better than a fish! The
Signora protests that the character in question
was that of a mermaid or syren. Then the bass
singer vows he will not sing save in pearl-coloured
stockings and red-heeled shoes. The fourth player
tells the audience that 'since the town was last
year so good as to encourage an opera without
singers' he trusts they will excuse them again and
'accept the proposal of the comedians, who rely
wholly on your courtesy and protection.'

The overture follows, and the first scene is the
house of Ducat, a West Indian trader, the action
of the play being wholly in the West Indies. The
songs are set, as in *The Beggar's Opera*, to popular
airs of the day—possibly not quite so good a
selection as in the previous opera. The old characters are Polly, Mrs Trapes, Jenny Diver, and
Macheath, who now figures under the name of
'Morano,' posing as a negro. He has blacked his
face and become captain of a pirate ship. Polly
Peachum is introduced to Ducat by Mrs Trapes,
for no good purpose. She denies that she has been
transported and mentions that 'the misfortunes

of her family' (hinting that her father has been hanged) and a search for Macheath her husband —transported—has brought her over to the West Indies. Mrs Trapes tells her that Macheath 'robbed his master, ran away from the plantation, and turned pirate.' Polly accepts service as maid to Mrs Ducat, but, seeing the trap she is in, seeks the aid of this lady to escape. There is now an alarm that the pirates are coming down and all is in an uproar. At this juncture an Indian enters and proclaims that his King will join forces with the English Colony in defence against the pirates. Ducat asks if Macheath is dead. The Indian replies that it is rumoured that he is, but that a negro named Morano is the chief of the pirates 'who in rapine and barbarities is even worse than he.' Polly begs Mrs Ducat to aid her in her escape from her husband and is dressed in a suit of youth's clothes by Mrs Ducat's contrivance.

The opening of the second act shows a view of the country, with Polly in boy's clothes. She falls asleep, when enter five men of the pirate gang. After drinking they dispute as to the division of the world they are about to conquer. One claims the whole kingdom of Mexico, and allots the isle of Cuba to his fellow, who will only be satisfied with Mexico. The clashing of swords awakens

Polly, who comes forward. They now take Polly with the intent to bring her before Morano.

Another scene shows Morano (Macheath) and Jenny Diver. She has not changed in character since her transportation, and Macheath's relations with her are as they were in England. We gather that it was she who persuaded Macheath to change his name and personality. She now proposes that he should rob the gang and fly with her to England. Vanderbluff, the lieutenant of the ship, reproaches Morano for his philandering with women, when the other members of the crew enter with Polly, still in boy's clothes, who is supposed to wish to join the gang. There is a scene in which Jenny Diver starts a flirtation with the supposed boy and denounces him to Morano. An interruption is caused by the gang bringing in a prisoner, the Chief of the Indians. Polly and the Indian are confined together. The tide of battle turns, and the Indians with the aid of the English Colony defeat the pirates and Morano is captured. Polly pleads for his life, but too late, as he is executed by the Indians. Polly now is to be married to the son of the Indian Chief, and the curtain falls.

The Indians are all highly moral, and voice sentiments of the highest degree of virtue, thus following the fashion of all eighteenth-century savages, Chinese philosophers, Turkish wise men, and the like—a convention to be excused on the plea that literary men of that day had never had experience of the real thing.

More than one edition of *Polly* appeared in 1729. The first was in quarto—*Polly, an opera, Being the second part of The Beggar's Opera written by Mr Gay*. This was printed for the author; it had an appendix of the tunes. There was also an octavo edition, *Printed for T. Thomson, and sold by the booksellers of London and Westminster*. This has the airs, not very well engraved, from copper plates on sixteen pages. There was also a Dublin edition of the music, in small folio from engraved copper plates—*The Whole Musick and songs of the Second Part of the Beggar's Opera, sett with basses proper for the violin harpsicord, or spinnet, carefully corrected from the London Edition*. This was published by John and William Neale about 1730, or 1735.

The musical arrangement of *Polly* appears to have been in the hands of Dr Pepusch.

## THE PUBLICATION OF *THE BEGGAR'S OPERA*

IT is not necessary to repeat the old saying that the opera made 'Rich gay, and Gay rich.' It is stated that Gay made £2000 as his share of the acting rights; another account gives it as near £700. Mr Charles E. Pearce had the good fortune to discover a copy of the original agreement by which Gay assigned to John Watts and Jacob Tonson, booksellers and printers, the copyright in *The Beggar's Opera* and in *The Fables*, for the sum of £94. 10s., dated 6th of February, 1727—really 1728, as the new year in those days did not take its right date before March; unless this particular chronology is realised, much confusion and many mistakes occur.

John Watts was the first printer of *The Beggar's Opera*, and also of the numerous ballad operas which followed it. His press was in Wild Court, Lincoln's Inn Fields, and it was with him that Benjamin Franklin worked as a journeyman, though before Watts printed the opera. The first edition of the opera is in octavo—*The Beggar's Opera, as it is acted at The Theatre Royal in*

# THE

# *BEGGAR's*

# OPERA.

As it is Acted at the

## THEATRE-ROYAL

### IN

## *LINCOLNS-INN-FIELDS.*

---

Written by Mr. *G A Y.*

---

——*Nos hæc novimus esse nihil.*    Mart.

---

To which is Added,

*The* MUSICK *Engrav'd on* COPPER-PLATES.

---

*LONDON:*

TITLE-PAGE OF *THE BEGGAR'S OPERA*
(FIRST EDITION)

*Lincoln's Inn Fields, written by Mr Gay, to which is added the musick engraved on copper plates; London, printed for John Watts* 1728, *price* 1s. 6d. The 'musick' is the airs rudely engraved on sixteen pages at the end of the book—the overture was not given. The second edition, with the overture, was printed also by Watts, but the music was now cut on woodblocks and inserted in the text. It is dated 1728. The third edition is printed by Watts in quarto in a manner much superior to the earlier ones; it is dated 1729, and the music, including the overture, is beautifully engraved, the airs having the basses. The music runs to forty-six pages. Another edition '*printed for J. & R. Tonson,*' dated 1765, is in octavo with an engraved frontispiece after F. Hayman. This is a reprint of the second edition, with the wooden music blocks inserted in the text. Some of these blocks are carelessly placed upside down. It has the overture also cut in wood. W. Strahan, who succeeded to this Watts and Tonson copyright in the opera, published editions, with the music, dated 1771 and 1777.

An edition of the music and words of the songs is entitled *The Excellent Choice, being a collection of the most favourite old Song Tunes in The Beggar's Opera set for 3 voices in the manner of Catches, or for two German flutes and a Bass. By Dr Pepusch,*

*and the most eminent English masters; London
printed for J. Walsh.* Oblong folio, *circ.* 1745–50,
51 pages. There are some of the airs omitted. A
fuller edition of the music is: *The Beggar's Opera
as it is performed at both Theatres, with the additional alterations and new basses by Dr Arne for
the voice, harpsichord, and violin.* Longman and
Broderip. Oblong folio. *Circ.* 1780. A year or
two later than this is the oblong folio edition,
following Dr Pepusch's arrangement, issued by
Harrison & Co., 18, Paternoster Row. A com-
panion volume in oblong folio by these publishers
is *Polly, an opera, being the Second Part of The
Beggar's Opera.* Oblong quarto editions of these
were also issued by Messrs Harrison, for the
German flute, at the same date.

Editions later than these, with and without the
music, are of course very numerous, and they
display the tamperings and omissions that the
opera was fated to suffer in Victorian times. One
of the most recent copies is a reprint of the 1765
edition with illustrations by the late C. Lovat
Fraser and an interesting foreword by him.

Of the indignities that the opera has received
there could be made a long list, but the following
will suffice. In 1777 a version by Captain Thomson was produced at Covent Garden with a view
to meeting the claims of the moral people who

thought that Macheath got off too lightly. The highwayman is sentenced to the Hulks on the Thames. He is here visited by Polly and Lucy and resolves to become a virtuous member of society. As the book was not printed we have no information how the rest of the plot was treated. The audience had the good taste to reject such a version.

*The Beggar's Opera* was translated into French by A. Hallam under the title *L'Opera du Gueux*. This was acted in Paris in 1750.

In the early nineteenth-century revivals of the opera, the three acts were condensed into two. When Sims Reeves took Macheath, there is no question that he was excellent in the part and sang the songs appropriate to the character with all the charm and voice that so enchanted the Victorian audiences of the seventies and eighties; but he introduced—no doubt by request of the managers—songs from his repertory, 'Tom Bowling,' 'Here's to the maiden of bashful fifteen,' and others, charming enough in the rendering of such a fine tenor, but an anachronism that, strictly speaking, might be open to censure. In this particular he may have very justly pleaded that he was but following an example such as Incledon, or Braham, might have set.

The opera has been performed in modern

clothes, notably with John Braham as Macheath in his every-day costume; and again with Madame Vestris as Macheath in a rakish top hat of the period; and other disquieting representations. Among these silly performances must be ranked one in which the male characters were enacted by women and Polly, Lucy, and the other ladies by full-grown men. Also another insult was a children's performance. Those who organised a child Macheath, Peachum, or Lockit, and a Diana Trapes had neither sense of art nor decency. Fortunately these last-named atrocities were confined to the eighteenth century.

Another item may be mentioned—*The Beggar's Pantomime, or the Contending Columbines,* having reference to a quarrel between Kitty Clive and Mrs Cibber over taking the character of Polly. The pantomime was a mere piece of fun with no ill intention; it was acted at Lincoln's Inn Fields in 1736.

After Sims Reeves had figured in the opera (his last appearance was in 1886), it does not seem to have been revived on the stage until the recent presentation at the Lyric Theatre, Hammersmith, under the supervision of Mr Nigel Playfair in 1920. The scenery and costumes were designed by the late Mr C. Lovat Fraser. The original music was charmingly arranged by Mr

SCENE FROM *THE BEGGAR'S OPERA*

Frederic Austin and the dances by Miss Marian Wilson. The opera itself appears to be too long for modern requirements; but, although there were certain necessary cuts, these were made so as not to injure the action of the piece, and in all probability the rendering was more like the original play, as Gay wrote it, than the representations in which Vestris, Braham, and Sims Reeves took part.

# PRODUCTION AND CRITICISM

*T*HE *Beggar's Opera* was produced at John Rich's theatre, Lincoln's Inn Fields, on January 29th, 1728 (or, according to the method of dating current at that period, 1727–8). It drew a fashionable crowd, many being political adherents of both parties. It is likely that these political spirits were somewhat disappointed, the one party that the political satire which is here and there apparent was of so general and so mild a character, the other party equally vexed that there was so little to lay hold of in a question of the suppression of the piece. Everybody knew that the Court and the Governing Party were corrupt, and the mere generalisation of this was nothing to complain of. Courts and Governments had been corrupt before, and politicians had robbed the public purse without scruple ever since the public had a purse to rob. The common audience did not notice any particular point at which to take up cudgels on behalf of politics. The brilliant dialogue, the wit, and life-like conception of the whole story appealed to them in a far greater degree than any flings at Court or Government.

The little pathetic picture of simple and trusting Polly Peachum amid an atmosphere of rascality was touching enough to the ordinary man and woman, and there can be but little doubt that Polly, with the charming acting of Lavinia Fenton, had the greatest influence upon the success of the piece. Miss Fenton, a young and obscure actress whom John Rich had just taken into his theatre, must have played the part of Polly with the artless simplicity that is such a contrast to the fierceness of Lucy Lockit, bred as she had been at the bar of a low tavern and living amid the corruption of Newgate. Miss Fenton's acting found its reward, as she attracted the attention of a duke and became Duchess of Bolton.

Thomas Walker made an effective Macheath; the part was originally intended for Quin. John Hippisley, originally a candle-snuffer in the theatre, played Peachum. He was all that could be desired in his part, and the like commendation may be given to John Hall, who played Lockit. In fact, Gay was fortunate in having so excellent a company for the play. Thomas Walker became a dissipated wreck in later life. He wrote at least a couple of ephemeral pieces, including *The Quaker's Opera*, which will be mentioned later; he died in Dublin in great distress in 1744. John Hippisley died at Bristol (where he had built a theatre) in 1748. The Duchess of Bolton (Miss Fenton) died a widow in January, 1760. Of the other characters nothing of importance has come down to us. In the original cast Mrs Peachum was played by Mrs Martin, Lucy Lockit by Mrs Egleton, and Filch by an actor named Clark.

It has been denied that *The Beggar's Opera* was written in ridicule of the Italian operas of the period, upon the assumption that it does not follow the lines of the Italian productions. It is, however, quite evident from the prologue between the Beggar and the Player that a rap at the Italian operas was intended. Besides which, there is a contemporary acceptance of the spirit of ridicule, for in the prologue to Colley Cibber's little piece, *Love in a Riddle*, acted in 1729, while *The Beggar's Opera* was in full glory, there is a passage:

> If songs are harmless revels of the heart,
> Why should our native tongue not bear its part?
> Why after learned warblers should we pant,
> And doat on airs which only they can chant?

And again in the Epilogue:

> Poor English mouths for twenty years
> Have been shut up from musick;
> But, thank our stars, outlandish airs
> At last have made all you sick.
> When warbling dames were all in flames
> And for precedence wrangled,
> One English play cut short the fray
> And home again they dangled.

Cibber's play was, like Gay's, interspersed with verses set to popular airs.

A poem by a writer named Lewis, published in 1730, entitled *Old England's Garland, or the Italian opera's downfall*, begins:

I sing of sad discords that happened of late,
Of strange revolutions, but not of the State,
How old England grew fond of old tunes of her own,
And her ballads went up and our operas went down.

All of which shows that the general public was tired of the Italian absorption of popular music, and that, if only on the score of bringing English tunes into recognition, Gay's opera was welcomed by the ordinary man. It has been mentioned before, on Pope's authority, that ladies had fans upon which the favourite songs and airs of the opera were printed. This is a proof that not only the vulgar appreciated them, but also the class that prided itself upon its taste. The collector of the odds and ends of a bygone period would no doubt esteem as precious a specimen of these *Beggar's Opera* fans, should such survive.

We can easily suppose that the upholders of the Italian banner did not take all this lying down, and for long after, even as late as the middle of the nineteenth century, there was much holding up of hands at the supposed immorality of the play. Sir John Hawkins in his *History of Music* has no stinted abuse. He says: 'The effects of *The Beggar's Opera* in the minds of the people have fulfilled the prognostications of many, that it would prove injurious to society. Rapine and violence have been gradually increasing ever since its first representation. The rights of property and the obligation of the laws that guard it are disputed upon principle. Everyman's house is now become, what the law calls it, his castle; or at least it may be said that, like a castle, it requires to be a place of defence. Young men, apprentices, clerks in public offices, and others, disdaining the arts of honest industry and captivated with the charms of idleness and criminal pleasures, now betake themselves to the road, affect politeness in the very act of robbery, and in the end become victims to the justice of their country. And men of discernment, who have been at the pains of tracing this great evil to its source, have found that not a few of those, who during these last fifty years have paid to the law the forfeit of their lives, have in the course of their pursuit been emulous to imitate the manners and general character of Macheath.'

This so covers the general adverse criticism of the eighteenth century that it is unnecessary to quote further. Dr Johnson with sounder sense said, 'As to this matter, which has been very much contested, I myself am of opinion, that more influence has been ascribed to *The Beggar's Opera*, than it in reality ever had; for I do not believe that any man was ever made a rogue by being present at its representation.' Boswell seems to have been one who saw a certain merit in it which the rest of the eighteenth century ignored, that is, as a picture of real life. He says: 'I should be very sorry to have *The Beggar's Opera* suppressed, for there is in it so much of real London life, so much brilliant wit, and such a variety of airs, which, from early association of ideas, engage, soothe, and enliven the mind, that no performance which the theatre exhibits, delights me more.' Here we get an appreciation of the true animus of the piece.

There is evidence to show that William Hogarth was also much taken with the opera. Its satire and protests against cruelty were sufficiently in his line of thought to appeal strongly to the painter of 'Marriage à la mode,' 'The Rake's Progress,' and the minor works which he engraved and published. He was friendly with the actors and designed several benefit tickets for them. One famous oil painting of his, of which he made one or two replicas, shows the stage with the stage-boxes filled with the notables who patronised the first performance. The scene is Newgate (and probably a fairly accurate view), with Macheath in the centre. On his right is Lucy Lockit appealing on her knees to her father, while on the other side is Polly in the same attitude at her father's feet.

Another work of Hogarth's is 'The Enraged Musician.' This depicts Castrucci, the leader of the Italian opera, at an open window, fiddle in hand, enraged at the noise of the street. A knife-grinder, a milk-maid, a pewterer, a postman with his horn, a chimney-sweep, a couple of cats on a roof, a yelping dog, and other characters all help to send the poor fiddler half crazy. The most bitter touch of all is a playbill of *The Beggar's Opera* pasted on the house side, on which can be read 'Mr Walker as Macheath, and Miss Fenton as Polly.' A beggar is bleating on a wind instrument (an oboe or similar instrument) while a woman ballad-singer is screeching at the top of her voice, the ballad which she holds for sale, 'The Ladies' Fall,' being perhaps a satirical touch at the ladies of the Italian opera whose songs were eclipsed by the simple ballad airs sung by Polly and Lucy.

George Hogarth, the musical critic of a later generation, refers to *The Beggar's Opera* in his *Musical History* (1835) as a 'profligate production ...said to have been intended to ridicule the Italian opera, which was then becoming very fashionable

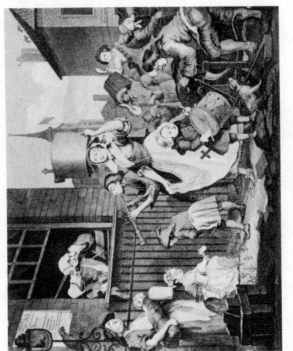

*THE ENRAGED MUSICIAN*

in England; though if this was its object, it certainly was not accomplished, as there is not the slightest resemblance in any particular between *The Beggar's Opera* and the pieces of the Italian stage.' He goes on to say that ' its still continuing to be performed, in defiance of public decency, says little for the boasted improvement in the morality of the stage.'

Whatever reason George Hogarth and those who thought with him may have had as to the desirability of keeping the opera off the stage, I have not seen or heard of any adverse criticism on the score of morality that the recent revival has brought forth. Whether we are less shocked at the representation of crime and general immorality than were our grandfathers is a matter uncertain; but I think many will grant that *The Beggar's Opera* stands well above a certain type of comedy that is not infrequent on the modern stage. Distance of period may of course have something to do with this, and also broadness of effect. At any rate, of the thousands who have seen the recent performances I have heard of none who have come away shocked.

## LATER BALLAD OPERAS

T has been suggested that Gay might have owed his inspiration to a play produced in 1725 called *The Prison Breaker, or the adventures of John Shephard*. At this time Shephard and his escapes from prison were much talked about. People admired his pluck and daring and there was much ephemeral literature regarding him.

The play was anonymous. Its scenes were chiefly in Newgate. The characters were Shephard, Jonathan Wile (evidently 'Wild'), and Rust, the Keeper of Newgate. There is Coax Thief, and his wife, several ladies of easy virtue, and a gang of thieves, associates of Shephard. The play has no wit and tries to get a comic element by the introduction of a Quaker, an Irishman, and a Welsh lawyer. After *The Beggar's Opera* had been first performed, Thomas Walker, the original Macheath, turned this play into *The Quaker's Opera*, and in 1728 it was performed at Lee and Harper's theatrical booth in Bartholomew Fair. It was published by 'J. W.' (John Watts), with the date 1728. Following the example set by Gay, a number of songs were introduced set to popular tunes. These tunes, cut in wood, are reproduced in Watts' edition. Among the airs was that afterwards used for 'The Miller of the Dee,' as well as the one associated with 'The Vicar of Bray,' here named 'The Country Garden.' Both these airs appear for the first time in print in this opera. Walker took the character of Shephard, probably not successfully, for he was a bulky man of some age, while the real Jack Shephard was a mere youth.

*The Quaker's Opera* was the first of the many ballad operas, following the lines of the *Beggar's,* that came forth in a flood after their prototype had shown the way to success. These operas were chiefly remarkable for their lack of wit and any other merit, save that of preserving old English tunes which, had not John Watts reproduced them in his editions, might have been lost to us. Watts was the chief publisher of the plays. They were all in octavo, chiefly with the airs cut in woodblocks inserted in the text. These octavo operas have considerable value to the student of English national song, as they contain, frequently for the first time in print, copies of our English national melodies, many which would otherwise have totally disappeared.

As in *The Beggar's Opera,* fresh sets of verses appropriate to the action of the play were written to the old tunes.

There was a rage for these ballad operas, poor as the quality was, between 1728 and 1733. They were acted at Drury Lane, Lincoln's Inn Fields, Goodman's Fields, etc. Copies are not now very common, but the following, almost all in the writer's possession, will give nearly a complete list of the ballad operas that succeeded *The Beggar's Opera*:

1728  *The Quaker's Opera.*
  „    *Penelope.*

1729  *Love in a Riddle* (by Colley Cibber).
  „    *The Beggar's Wedding.*
  „    *The Cobler's Opera.*
  „    *Flora, or Hob in the Well.*
  „    *The Lover's Opera.*
  „    *Momus turned Fabulist, or Vulcan's Wedding.*
  „    *The Patron.*
  „    *The Village Opera.*
  „    *Damon and Phillida.* (An alteration of Colley Cibber's *Love in a Riddle*.)
  „    *The Wedding.*

1730  *Robin Hood.* (This was probably by Thomas Walker. Like *The Quaker's Opera*, it was acted at Lee and Harper's booth in Bartholomew Fair.)
  „    *The Female Parson, or Beau in the Sudds.*

1730  *The Chambermaid.*

   ,,    *Patie and Peggy, or The Fair Foundling.*
        (A condensed version of Ramsay's *Gentle Shepherd.*)

   ,,    *The Fashionable Lady, or Harlequin's Opera.*

1731  *The Highland Fair, or the Union of the Clans.*

   ,,    *The Devil to pay, or Wives Metamorphos'd.*

   ,,    *The Lottery.*

   ,,    *The Jovial Crew.*

   ,,    *The Generous Freemason, or The Constant Lady.*

   ,,    *Silvia, or The Country Burial.*

   ,,    *The Beggar's Wedding.*

1732  *The Devil of a Duke, or Trapolin's Vagaries.*

   ,,    *The Mock Doctor, or The Dumb Lady Cured.*

1733  *The Boarding School, or The Sham Captain.*

   ,,    *The Decoy.*

   ,,    *The Livery Rake.*

   ,,    *The Mad Captain.*

   ,,    *The Fancy'd Queen.*

   ,,    *Achilles.* (By Gay.)

1734  *The Intriguing Chambermaid.*

1735  *An old man taught wisdom, or The virgin unmask'd.*

   ,,    *Trick for Trick.*

1735 *The Merry Cobler* (sequel to *The Devil to pay*).

1737 *The Rival Milliners, or The humours of Covent Garden.*

The above is a fairly full, if not a complete, list of the early eighteenth-century ballad operas, in which the same method of using old or popular airs as in *The Beggar's Opera* was employed.

After the last given date, 1737, the practice appeared to cease until 1762, when *Love in a Village*, founded on *The Village Opera* of 1729, was produced. *Midas* (1764) and a whole host of others followed, in which the tunes were partly composed and partly selected by the arrangers.

This second epoch of the English opera, in which Storace, Dr Arnold, Shield, and others were employed, is full of interest but rather outside the limits of the present volume.

# INDEX